AGENTS OF CHANGE

Internal Auditors in the Era of Permacrisis

Second Edition

RICHARD F. CHAMBERS, CIA, CFE, CRMA

with ROBERT PEREZ

Sponsored by

FINA PRESS

Copyright © 2021, 2024 by Richard F. Chambers & Associates. All rights reserved.

Published by Fina Press, an imprint of Wow Media Publishing Consultants, LLC

No part of this publication may be reproduced, stored in a retrieval system, or transmitted in any form by any means—electronic, mechanical, photocopying, recording, or otherwise— without prior written permission of the publisher. Requests to the publisher for permission should be sent electronically to: wowmediapublishing@outlook.com with the subject line "reprint permission request."

Limit of Liability: Fina Press publishes this document for informational and educational purposes and is not a substitute for legal or accounting advice. The publisher does not provide such advice and makes no warranty as to any legal or accounting results through its publication of this document. When legal or accounting issues arise, professional assistance should be sought and retained.

The IIA's International Professional Practices Framework (IPPF) comprises the full range of existing and developing practice guidance for the profession. The IPPF provides guidance to internal auditors globally and paves the way to world-class internal auditing.

The 2024 edition of this book is sponsored by AuditBoard.

AuditBoard is the leading cloud-based platform in transforming audit, risk, compliance, and ESG management. Nearly 50% of the Fortune 500 leverage AuditBoard to move their businesses forward with greater clarity and agility.

Print: 978-1-963998-00-9
ePub: 978-1-963998-01-6

24 25 26 27 28 LSI 10 9 8 7 6 5 4 3 2 1

Acknowledgments

Writing the 2nd edition of this book has been another rewarding experience in my journey to inform and inspire the global profession of internal auditing. Once again, it would not have been possible without the encouragement and support of so many family members, friends, and colleagues.

I must first acknowledge the extraordinary efforts of my writing partner, Robert Pérez. His vision, energy, and tireless dedication to both the original edition and this 2nd edition were critical to its success. Robert helped me find my voice in my articles, blogs, and books for the last 7 years I was IIA President and CEO. He was the first person I asked to assist me with the first edition of this book, and I would not have undertaken this edition had he not said yes to reprising his role.

My wife, Kim, has been a vital partner who has been inspiring me to be a change agent for more than 30 years. She is a source of encouragement and support each time I write a book. Her words of advice, reassurance, patience, and understanding were vital to undertaking such demanding projects. My talented and beautiful daughters, Natalie McElwee, Christina Morton, and Allison Chambers have always been unwavering in their affection and support. As I grow older, I am also motivated by my three grandchildren, Kennedy, MacKenzie, and Luke. They help me maintain a healthy perspective on life.

Thank you to AuditBoard, Inc., for sponsoring this edition and for their unwavering support over the past three years. Thanks to Scott Garner and Lucio Peralta for their extraordinary work on the cover design of this edition. Thanks also to Scott Arnold for the kind words he shared in the foreword to this edition.

Agents of Change: Internal Auditors in an Era of Disruption was the last book I authored as president and CEO of The IIA, In that edition, I thanked all of the men and women in volunteer leadership roles during my years of service who modeled the change agent attributes explored in this book. I am particularly grateful for the unwavering support I have received from the 13 men and women who chaired The IIA's Board of Directors during my 12-year tenure: Patty Miller, 2008–2009; Rod Winters, 2009–2010; Gunther Meggeneder, 2010–2011; Denny Beran, 2011–2012; Phil Tarling, 2012–2013; Paul Sobel, 2013–2014; Anton van Wyk, 2014–2015; Larry Harrington, 2015–2016; Angela Witzany, 2016–2017; Mike Peppers, 2017–2018; Naohiro Mouri (Mouri-san), 2018–2019; Mike Joyce, 2019–2020; and Jenitha John, 2020–2021.

About the Authors

Richard F. Chambers, CIA, CFE, QIAL, is one of the leading voices and thought leaders in the internal audit profession. He has spent almost 50 years serving and supporting the internal audit profession, including more than 12 years as president and CEO of The Institute of Internal Auditors (IIA). He currently works as Senior Internal Audit Advisor for AuditBoard and heads his own internal audit advisory and training firm, Richard F. Chambers and Associates, LLC.

Prior to leading The IIA, Richard was national practice leader of Internal Audit Advisory Services at PwC; inspector general of the Tennessee Valley Authority; deputy inspector general of the U.S. Postal Service; and director of the U.S. Army Worldwide Internal Review Organization at the Pentagon.

An award-winning blogger and highly sought after speaker, Richard has authored three award-winning books: Trusted Advisors: Key Attributes of Outstanding Internal Auditors (2017), The Speed of Risk: Lessons Learned on the Audit Trail, 2nd Edition (2019), and Agents of Change: Internal Auditors in an Era of Disruption (2021).

Richard and his wife, Kim, reside in New Smyrna Beach, Florida, and have three daughters, Natalie, Christina, and Allison.

Robert Pérez is an award-winning writer who has spent more than four decades as a professional journalist, editor, and strategic communicator. A former director of content development and delivery at The IIA, Robert helped shape communication strategy and thought leadership to support internal audit practitioners globally. He was part of IIA teams that produced the annual *North American Pulse of Internal Audit* report, *OnRisk* guide, and the American Corporate Governance Index. He helped create and launch The IIA's award-winning *All Things Internal Audit* podcast, as well as other video and audio content for the organization.

Prior to joining The IIA in 2014, Robert was vice president of CBR Public Relations. Earlier in his career, he spent more than 25 years as a journalist at several newspapers, including the *Orlando Sentinel*, the *Dallas Times Herald*, and *The Wall Street Journal.*

Robert and his wife, Barbara, reside in the Orlando, Florida, area.

Foreword

I am honored to introduce the second edition of Richard Chambers' latest book, *Agents of Change: Internal Auditors in the Era of Permacrisis*. I first met Richard as he was leaving his role as President and CEO of The Institute of Internal Auditors (IIA) after twelve years of significant change. Initially, we connected over a shared passion for technology and its ability to enable value in organizations. What became crystal clear to me was Richard's deep passion to elevate the profession and his desire to collaborate with like-minded organizations. Our partnership seemed destined and, soon enough, we had joined forces with AuditBoard sponsoring the first edition of *Agents of Change*.

In the three short years since our partnership began, I have marveled at Richard's true passion to live as an agent of change. He has spent countless hours engaging with professionals across audit, risk management, and compliance roles listening to their challenges and encouraging them to be bold, to take risks, and to set the bar higher for themselves and their teams. He does this in powerful, yet simple ways — being available for questions after a keynote, signing books and taking pictures with those who admire his work, and personally sharing his deep experience and challenges. He also magnifies their voices through video series and other media, even as he speaks clearly with his own. He challenges every practitioner to take the next right step in embracing change as an opportunity to enhance their strategic impact.

This revelatory update of *Agents of Change* comes at a compelling moment in time — during a shift from the era of post-COVID disruption that characterized the first edition into a period of persistent crisis, a "permacrisis" as Richard has coined it. Today's risks are more complex, interdependent, and growing at an exponential rate as both the volume and velocity of risk explode. Unfortunately, most organizations are not able to grow resources to keep pace, even as the cost of risk events grows seemingly unbounded. The resulting frustration and challenge for professionals is one that Richard feels deeply and is working to help solve.

Throughout his storied career, Richard has continued to challenge himself, learn, and elevate his thinking even as he has become perhaps the most recognized voice for audit on the planet. Richard's first two books, *Lessons Learned on the Audit Trail* and *Trusted Advisors: Key Attributes of Outstanding Internal Auditors*, share Richard's extensive experience and provide a practical guide to honing the practice of audit for individuals and their teams while modernizing audit approaches for today's dynamic organizations. In these pages, Richard builds on those ideas to challenge all practitioners to accept change across every dimension of their work as inevitable and an opportunity to embrace innovation, leverage new technology, and envision the big picture in fresh and impactful ways. In so doing, a practitioner can become an agent of change.

No one embodies the spirit of this conviction and change better than Richard Chambers as he demonstrates through the numerous practical suggestions contained herein. He also shares a cautionary warning that auditors who remain behind the barriers of independence and objectivity, unwilling to accept the new reality, risk losing relevance in their organizations. With challenges such as rapid digital transformation, geopolitical conflicts, expansion of third-party risks, and the commercialization of new technologies including generative AI, business leaders need internal auditors more than ever for assurance and guidance to make risk-informed strategic decisions.

For internal auditors especially, this moment represents an exciting opportunity to prove their value as trusted advisors to be sure, but also as a vanguard of change agents with fresh perspectives, clear strategic insights, and the ability to leverage technology as a powerful force-multiplier. This is where I see Richard's heart most clearly, and his passion is on full display as he helps empower a generation of audit, risk, and compliance leaders to accept this challenge.

Foreword

As Richard champions the message of uniting audit, risk, and compliance professionals in collaboration across their organizations, this second edition of *Agents of Change: Internal Auditors in the Era of Permacrisis* is a "must read" for anyone seeking to elevate their impact and the profession. I can't wait for you to read it.

Scott Arnold
President and CEO, AuditBoard

Contents

Acknowledgments i
About the Authors iii
Foreword v
Introduction xi

Part 1: A Legacy of Change

Chapter 1: The Imperative for Change 1
Chapter 2: Responding to Risk in Permacrisis 17
Chapter 3: Independence Doesn't Imply Isolation 27

Part Two: Enacting the Change

Chapter 4: Agent Change Thyself 47
Chapter 5: Driving Change 61
Chapter 6: Leveraging Enabling Technology 73
Chapter 7: Agents of Change Aren't Secret Agents 87

Part Three: The Right Stuff

Chapter 8: Business Acumen 103
Chapter 9: The Strategic Internal Auditor 117
Chapter 10: On Being Relationship Centric 131
Chapter 11: The Innovative Mindset 145
Conclusion: Agents of the Future 157

Notes 163

Introduction

Robert Pérez and I collaborated on the first edition of this book (*Agents of Change: Internal Auditors in an Era of Disruption*) during the dark and uncertain year following the onset of the COVID pandemic. We made a number of references to the unprecedented disruption being wrought by the pandemic as it was unfolding. However, neither of us would fully come to appreciate the transformational change the pandemic itself would have until after the book was published.

Agents of Change was my third original manuscript, and in each edition, I have been able to reflect on the dynamic nature of internal audit and the evolution the profession has undergone.

Lessons Learned on the Audit Trail (first edition) was a semi-autobiographical book about my experiences over nearly 40 years in the internal audit profession. I wanted to impart a bit of wisdom based on my exposure to hundreds, if not thousands, of audits and internal auditors who shaped my views of risk, independent assurance, good governance, and the value that internal audit provides. Five years later, I offered an updated look at the audit trail in a second edition to the original manuscript, titled *The Speed of Risk*.

One of the chapters in *Lessons Learned on the Audit Trail* touched on becoming a trusted advisor. I have long preached the value of building relationships with our stakeholders — on the board, in the C-suite, and across the organization — to help elevate internal audit and earn a seat at the table with management and others. This is possible only by demonstrating conclusively and consistently how internal audit helps an organization achieve its goals. The abbreviated examination of some key characteristics of proven trusted advisors provided the genesis for my second book.

For *Trusted Advisors: Key Attributes of Outstanding Internal Auditors*, I surveyed and interviewed an array of leading internal auditors. From those discussions, I gleaned insights into the traits that characterize outstanding internal auditors — those individuals who have earned that seat at the table and are also considered trusted advisors in their organizations. I examined attributes including ethical resiliency, critical thinking, business acumen, intellectual curiosity, dynamic communication skills, and insightful relationship building.

While *Lessons Learned on the Audit Trail* was a retrospective on our roles as assurance and advisory providers, *Trusted Advisors* was a contemporary look at the profession and the traits that leading internal auditors demonstrate in building and sustaining trust. While exploring the past and the present is important, we will never realize our full potential until we look forward. That is where the first edition of this book, *Agents of Change: Internal Auditors in an Era of Disruption*, took readers.

Since the first edition of this book was published in early 2021, the world has experienced one of the most consistently disruptive periods in its history. Constant upheaval from a pandemic, geopolitical instability, financial institution failures, and disruptive AI technology have created a wildly unpredictable risk landscape. The 2020s is being aptly described as the "era of permacrisis," because the world is seemingly gyrating through an endless stream of risk-induced disruption. If ever the world needed change agents, it's in the era of permacrisis. Thus, the title of this edition was born: *"Agents of Change: Internal Auditors in the Era of Permacrisis."*

What Is an Agent of Change?

My intent is for this edition of the book to be a beacon that shines the light on imperatives and opportunities for internal audit practitioners at all levels. To truly impart value to our organizations, we must be catalysts for transformation that creates value within the organizations we serve. To be sure, we add value when our assurance engagements identify corrective measures that need to be undertaken in the wake of audit findings. We certainly add value when we impart advice as our organizations' trusted advisors. But our objectives should not be limited to providing assurance and advice. More importantly,

Introduction

we should be influencing positive change that enhances our organizations' value. This is even more vital when our organizations are being subjected to the external forces brought on by permacrisis.

I first wrote about internal auditors as agents of change in a 2015 blog post. In the years since, I have often urged internal auditors to embrace the role and join other catalysts in their organizations who thrive on change and innovation. We have a unique seat at our organizations' table. It is often a seat that affords a 360-degree view of the risks and opportunities facing our stakeholders. We have become adept at highlighting the risks. We must become equally comfortable shining a light on opportunities.

In preparing to write the first edition of this book, I embraced the same approach I used when writing *Trusted Advisors*. I had my own ideas on how internal auditors can drive change and what it takes to be successful. But I didn't want the book to reflect only my point of view. So, once again, I went to the most reliable source of knowledge of what agents of change are all about — change agents themselves. Working with the Internal Audit Foundation, we surveyed almost 600 chief audit executives (CAEs) and internal audit directors around the world on what it takes to be an agent of change in twenty-first century internal auditing. The results were revealing and provided the basis for this book.

As we did for *Trusted Advisors*, we followed up our survey with in-depth conversations with CAEs who clearly model what it takes to be agents of change. The survey feedback and interviews were very instructive in organizing this book. In preparing this edition, we closely examined the key trends and important lessons learned in the post-COVID era of permacrisis. We have updated the first edition to explore the challenges of identifying emerging risks; deploying systems for continuous risk monitoring; the phenomenon of agile auditing; the incredible opportunities and ominous risk presented by artificial intelligence; and the ability of organizational culture to facilitate or impede the work of change agents.

As with the first edition, *Agents of Change: Internal Auditors in an Era of Permacrisis* comprises three parts that make the case for becoming change agents, emphasize that internal auditors must start by changing themselves, and articulate the skills embedded in change agents' DNA. Specifically:

Part One: A Legacy of Change

Modern internal auditors are a product of centuries of change. Indeed, the profession has been in constant evolution since its inception. The era of permacrisis has further exacerbated the imperative to audit at the speed of risk. Permacrisis is characterized by ambiguity, complexity, and virtually incomprehensible events. These are concepts that now play oversized roles in our lives and our work in the future. Tomorrow's leaders will be those who can quickly decipher complex threats and recognize opportunities in crisis. The change agents among us will have to possess a level of acceptance or comfort with what is unknowable.

Part Two: Enacting the Change

Before internal auditors can be indispensable agents of change within our organizations, we must change ourselves. We can no longer embrace processes rooted in the past century if we are to be taken seriously by those we serve in this one. We must bring an agile mindset to the way we execute our mission so that we are truly adept at auditing at the speed of risk. We are often thwarted in our efforts to drive change by the organizational cultures in which we operate. The proliferation of AI is presenting extraordinary opportunities and also daunting risks. To be change agents, we must have a keen understanding of each. Perhaps most importantly, we must become adept at telling our story. We cannot expect others to envision our potential if we keep our heads down and mouths shut.

Part Three: The Right Stuff

The most valuable insights from our global survey were the feedback on the common characteristics of agents of change. Respondents rated the importance of 14 characteristics, and we identified four common traits that distinguish great change agents from the rest. First, they possess strong business acumen and have a keen understanding of their organizations. Second, they bring a strategic mindset to everything they do—starting with their strategy for internal audit itself. Third, strong agents of change are relationshipcentric. They recognize that their success in influencing and inspiring change must be rooted in strong, resilient relationships. Fourth, agents of change are innovative. They aren't content with recycling the same solutions. They are purveyors of solutions that drive change and enhance organizational value.

Trusted Advisors versus Change Agents

By now you may be wondering — what is the difference between a trusted advisor and an agent of change? By my definitions, it is not an either/or proposition. Trusted advisors build and sustain trust from those they serve, and the recommendations and advice they offer are valued and embraced by their stakeholders. As I noted earlier, agents of change are catalysts for transformation that creates value within their organizations. They also must be trusted advisors, but not all trusted advisors are agents of change. Trusted advisors are often fulfilled by being heard, while agents of change are fulfilled by inspiring transformation that enhances value.

Internal auditors used to be derisively referred to as "bean counters." The classic assurance providers in the profession still count the beans. Trusted advisors, on the other hand, know how to grow, harvest, and take the beans to market. But it is the change agents in the profession who are bold and confident enough to advocate changing the crops from growing beans to growing corn.

I hope this book will inform and inspire you to become a catalyst for transformation within your organization.

Part 1

A Legacy of Change

Chapter 1

The Imperative for Change

It is not the strongest of the species that survive, nor the most intelligent, but the one most responsive to change.

— Charles Darwin —

I am often asked for the one piece of advice I would give to someone new to the internal audit profession. The answer has been the same for almost two decades: Follow the risks. My reasoning is that we add the greatest value to our organizations when we allocate our scarce, highly skilled talents to the most significant risks — the events that can potentially disrupt or prevent our organizations from attaining their objectives.

It is easy enough to simply say "follow the risks." But it is critically important for internal auditors to understand how risk influences strategies and decisions that executive management and boards make to create and sustain value in our organizations.

These components should feed our understanding of risk, our biases about how risks should be managed, and our views on how internal audit can provide value to organizations. But even as these factors complicate an already unimaginably complex web of risks that affect today's organizations, the work of internal audit comes down to a simple truth first articulated in *La Logique ou l'Art de Penser (Logic, or the Art of Thinking)*, published in 1662:

> *"Fear of harm ought to be proportional not merely to the gravity of the harm but also to the probability of the event."*

This is a fundamental concept in risk management — balancing impact and likelihood. Yet, while the work of modern internal auditing is all about risk, we spend surprisingly little time trying to understand our relationship with it, though that relationship is as old as humankind itself.

As long as humans have existed, we have had to manage risk — so much so that risk is embedded in our DNA. I refer to the "fight-or-flight" response built into our brains to handle a perceived or real threat. However, outside of this instinctive response, humans have developed a more sophisticated relationship with risk, one that is built on calculating probabilities and potential rewards. Peter L. Bernstein notes in his 1996 book, *Against the Gods: The Remarkable Story of Risk*, that the word risk derives from the early Italian word risicare, which actually means "to dare." He writes:

> *"In this sense, risk is a choice rather than a fate. The actions we dare to take, which depend on how free we are to make choices, are what the story of risk is all about. And that story helps define what it means to be a human being."*[1]

This choice to dare is at the heart of modern business theory and something all internal auditors must understand and embrace. The risk/reward concept takes on many forms, from racecar drivers who pit their skills against the risk of serious injury or death to businesses that invest in developing new products or venture into new markets to boost sales and profits.

From an organizational perspective, effectively managing risk — whether external or self-imposed — is fundamental to good governance. What's more, the assurance that an independent and objective internal audit function provides over the effectiveness of risk management is a critical component of sound governance.

While "follow the risk" is the most common piece of advice I give internal auditors, the second most frequent is "adapt to meet the needs and expectations of stakeholders." In fact, "adapting" has been a common theme throughout the history of our profession. Internal auditing in the twenty-first century bears little resemblance to the profession in its early origins. The value being delivered by the profession today is the product of a legacy of change dating back centuries.

For as long as modern internal audit has existed, organizations have steered the profession to best fit their most pressing risk management needs. That primarily focused on assurance over financial reporting in the post Great Depression era and through the end of the 20th Century. Indeed, the profession's evolution has been influenced greatly by visceral reactions to scandal.

That was abundantly evident in the first 10 years of the twenty-first century, as well, as major scandals shook the financial world. It began with the Enron and World-Com debacles, which led to the landmark U.S. Sarbanes-Oxley Act of 2002. That legislation was jokingly referred to as the Internal Auditor Full Employment Act because of the bevy of new regulations that broadly expanded financial reporting compliance risks. As late as 2023, financial reporting compliance accounted for more than 30% of the typical publicly traded company's internal audit plan in the United States.[2] Meanwhile, as the globe was thrust into the Great Recession, banking scandals led to development of the U.S. Dodd-Frank Wall Street Reform and Consumer Protection Act in 2010.

Beyond their impact on regulations, high-profile corporate scandals this century have fed a growing recognition that culture is often at the core of scandal, and that internal audit has a role to play in assessing culture. Many inside and outside the profession have expressed doubts about internal audit's ability to audit culture effectively, but the profession is making great progress in this area. I address culture's influence on our ability to become agents of change in Chapter 5.

However, the greatest change in internal audit's direction in the past 30 years has been the advent of the digital age and the relentless pull of innovation and technology. Beyond its disruptive influence on business models the digital age introduced the menacing and ubiquitous threat of cyberattacks. While cyber threats in the form of computer viruses have existed since the 1980s, the threat of widespread cyberattacks on business and industry became a reality in the 1990s as the world went online. In the three decades since, cybersecurity has risen to the peak of the risk management iceberg.

The emergence of the novel COVID-19 pandemic in early 2020 opened a Pandora's Box of business continuity, crisis management, supply chain, and new cyber vulnerabilities. This tested the profession's ability to provide effective assurance under the most challenging conditions. Again, the profession adapted. At astounding speeds, internal audit leaders and practitioners around the globe adjusted their processes and innovated new ways of auditing remotely or with dramatically limited on-site access. What's more, they generally thrived during the global emergency and were able to demonstrate value to their organizations.

But even as the world labored to eventually emerge from the pandemic's deadly malaise, technology's march continued unabated. In late 2022, the introduction of publicly accessible tools that use generative artificial intelligence (AI) planted the seeds for the next evolution, indeed revolution, in business opportunities and risks.

It is significant that the profession has successfully pivoted to meet the changing demands of a dynamic risk landscape, and I would be remiss in not acknowledging the critical role of The Institute of Internal Auditors (IIA) in shaping that success.

One of the most significant contributions to support the evolution of the profession in response to the volatile and dynamic risk landscape was the addition of Core Principles for the Professional Practice of Internal Auditing to the 2017 update to the International Professional Practices Framework (IPPF). But the change is more than just an addition or update to the profession's guidelines. The 10 principles articulate the fundamental beliefs that drive the internal audit profession. Those guideposts are designed to help practitioners remain centered on the core philosophies of internal auditing, even as technology, climate, geo- politics, macroeconomics, and social norms change the world around us.

The IIA's new Global Internal Audit Standards, introduced in early 2024, incorporated those principles into its five Domains—internal audit's purpose, ethics and professionalism, governing the internal audit function, managing the internal audit function, and performing internal audit services.

The IIA's guidance has inexorably moved the profession toward its rightful place as a trusted advisor to management, an equal partner in risk management, and a fundamental component of sound corporate governance. For several years, The IIA's strategic plan incorporated a 2030 vision statement, which set as an objective having the profession "universally recognized as indispensable to effective governance, risk management, and control."

Domain I of the IIA Standards provides a new Purpose of Internal Auditing that reflects the progress we've made toward achieving that original 2030 vision statement. The Purpose of Internal Auditing states in part:

> Internal auditing strengthens the organization's ability to create, protect, and sustain value by providing the board and management with independent, risk-based, and objective assurance, advice, insight, and foresight.

What's more, The IIA announced its Vision 2035 project in 2023 which, "is designed to envision the future state of the Internal Audit profession and chart the steps necessary to make that future a reality."[3]

The Core Principles, Purpose of Internal Auditing, and Vision 2035 all are vital parts of the profession steadily marching forward to a drumbeat of change. It should be a point of pride for all internal auditors that we have made palpable progress toward that lofty goal of becoming indispensable to good governance. But truly achieving it will require further evolution and a mind-set that motivates internal auditors to become agents of change.

A Natural Evolution

Looking back at the history of internal auditing, it's clear the profession has never been static. Indeed, our evolution has been extraordinary. As we look forward, we need to consider the next leap in terms of our value proposition. Embracing challenges and opportunities amid the chaos of near constant change is that next leap.

While at times it may seem like for every step we take forward we take two steps back, there is an unmistakable trajectory of progress. New challenges are a call to action to step forward — wherever they may take us. In that sense, we are not at all different from other professions. The medical profession has evolved from diagnosing and treating symptoms to developing preventative medicines and encouraging lifestyles that keep people healthier and more resilient and resistant to disease.

So it is with internal auditing. We must provide our organizations with the insight and foresight to not only protect value but help them fulfill their mandate to create value for their investors and stakeholders. Becoming true agents of change is part of the natural evolution of internal audit.

Consider this: when I assumed my first internal audit role in 1975, the most sophisticated technology in the department was a 10-key calculator, and our data was maintained on 16-column paper pads. We had no fax machine, and desktop and laptop computers were still more than a decade away. Our audit plans were based on a predetermined list of activities and departments that needed to be audited every two to three years. Oh, how the internal audit profession has changed! The profession changed because it was imperative that it evolve, and that imperative is likely to drive even more dramatic change in the decade(s) ahead.

As we have seen, there are many factors driving the evolution of internal auditing. For the lion's share of its history, change has happened at a deliberate, methodical pace. The forces of technology and disruption were kept in check by limits on communications, transportation, and science. Part of the challenge of the twenty-first century is that these limits are effectively gone. One example is the evolution in mobile connectivity, known as 5G. The impact has been nothing as pedestrian as faster download speeds; 5G now fuels a "connected everything" world. Connected cars, smart communities, industrial internet of things (IoT), immersive education — these and more were made possible by 5G.

This transformative technology has increased the volume of data coming into organizations from billions of bytes of data, known as gigabytes, to trillions of gigabytes, known as zettabytes. Indeed, according to published reports, the amount of data generated annually is growing exponentially, with one estimate calculating that 90% of the world's data was created since 2021. For example, there was about two zettabytes of data created in 2010. That figure was 120 zettabytes in 2023 and that figure is expected to grow to 181 zettabytes in 2025.[4]

When 5G was introduced, it was difficult to grasp the enormity of its potential, but it was easy to predict that organizations would leverage the powerful new business tool. And so, it has come to pass. Real-time monitoring of production lines, predictive maintenance and enhanced supply chain management is transforming efficiencies in manufacturing. Wearable technologies are making remote patient monitoring commonplace. The technology has seamlessly worked its way into our daily lives, whether it's ordering a driverless Waymo taxi in Phoenix or San Francisco or conversing with a human-like chatbot enabled by advanced natural-language processing applications.

The tsunami of data enabled by 5G creates a classic risk/opportunity conundrum: Collecting, analyzing, understanding, managing, protecting, and auditing today's data already poses logistical, resource, and talent problems for many organizations. Imagine what it will be like when data streams expand exponentially. Cybersecurity challenges, already a significant concern, are expected to multiply. Complicating the issue is a growing global data privacy movement.

However, the challenge for modern organizations and governments is to not merely survive 5G and other disruptive firestorms but to thrive amid these conflagrations. The reward for those that do is that, just as iron is strengthened by a tempering process, organizations will emerge stronger, more agile, and resilient enough to manage the next firestorm. Just as tempering makes metals less brittle, organizations must learn to manage stress without breaking.

As an integral component to effective risk management and sound governance, internal auditors must become agents of change who support and instigate the tempering process within their organizations. We must expose weaknesses, question conclusions (such as on data), challenge ill-conceived strategies, and promote actions that help create and enhance value. However, to become true agents of change, we must understand and accept the urgency of the moment and realize and take immediate action to overcome our own weaknesses.

Where Internal Audit Is Lagging

The imperative for change in the internal audit profession is rooted in the challenges and complexities wrought by technological disruption and the accelerating velocity of risks. These factors demand assurance and advice that is insightful, prescient, relevant, and trusted. However, in its present state, the profession is not positioned to deliver.

Risk management is difficult. Organizations continually face extraordinary headwinds spawned by a turbulent environment in which risks materialize seemingly overnight. In the second decade of the century, global financial and business markets were rocked by spectacular cybersecurity breaches, corporate failures induced by toxic cultures, and the fallout of sexual assault and harassment in the workplace. The early years of the third decade ushered in a powerful social justice movement, the accelerating effects of climate change, and myriad impacts on economic, cyber, business continuity, and talent-management risks brought on by the global COVID-19 pandemic. And just as the world was regaining its footing after the historic plague, science and technology was ready with a new and powerful disruptor—artificial intelligence. While all that may seem extraordinary, it's evident that risk events once thought of as black swans are increasingly becoming routine.

Outdated Processes

Internal auditors must realize and accept that the profession's bread-and-butter processes—annual risk assessments; rigid, risk-based annual audit plans; lengthy audit engagements; verbose, narrative-driven reports—are relics that position practitioners to only address yesterday's challenges. This reinforces my long-held belief that internal audit must take a continuous approach to risk assessment and assurance — auditing at the speed of risk.

Lisa Lee, vice president of audit at Alphabet/Google, laments that even in an organization considered progressive, there can be a tendency for internal audit reports to tell the *how* and not the *why*.

"It never fails: A first draft of any audit report still seems to focus on what we did," Lee said. "Why does that matter? Why should the business care about the work that we did? What matters is the value from insights we bring to them."

Adopting New Technology in Audit Processes

Research also continues to point to a troubling truth about the profession's relationship with technology: It's broken. Despite years of admonitions from The IIA and other leading internal audit voices, the adoption of technology to improve internal audit efficiency remains low. Foot-dragging on technology is reflected in the profession's continuing struggle to provide assurance to their organizations.

PwC's Global Internal Audit Study 2023 offers encouraging information about the demand for agents of change. The study's survey of business leaders found that nearly 7 in 10 (68%) want greater strategic engagement from internal audit in risk identification and assessment and more than half seek internal audit's involvement in management strategy and planning. This is great news! Yet, when asked to identify the strongest attributes of their internal audit departments, fewer than 2 in 10 (19%) identified data analytics skills including visualization as a strength. Just as troubling, the same percentage of respondents (19%) identified strategic thinking, and creative thinking, flexibility and agility as strengths.

The study found: ". . . nearly a third of IA leaders report they are not using data and technology to a great extent in any area, including scoping or testing activities in individual audits."[5]

Similarly, Protiviti's 2023 Next-Generation Internal Audit Survey describes investments in data and enabling technologies as, "key drivers of internal audit transformation. These technology tools also play a central role in building the function's relevance with the board, senior executives and stakeholders throughout the organization. . . All of this makes the internal audit function's use of technology critical to its success and this is an area notably in need of improvement, from a capabilities perspective." [6]

As risks grow more complex with every new technological disruption, stakeholders are demanding more from internal audit. Reports such as the ones from Protiviti and PwC suggest the profession may not be able to meet those demands.

We must ask ourselves two key questions:

- Why is where we are today not good enough?
- What can we do about it?

Our Trusted Processes Can't Keep Up with the Speed of Risk

Internal audit must make a concerted and coordinated effort to modernize its processes and approach to assurance and advisory services. COVID-19 increased awareness of the need for more frequent updates, not just to audit plans but also to risk assessments. Indeed, 6 in 10 internal auditors globally said their functions updated audit plans, identified emerging risks, and reviewed risk assessments in the wake of the fast-spreading coronavirus, according to three IIA surveys conducted in the first months after a pandemic was declared.

Part of any revolution must include a change in how we adapt and adopt technology. For example, the profession is slow to embrace the use of robotics process automation (RPA) and artificial intelligence (AI). Those will be vital tools if we hope to not just manage but understand and leverage the tidal wave of data available because of 5G and other still-unseen technological advances.

The Internal Audit Mindset Is to Pivot to Change, Not Anticipate or Initiate It

I have written and spoken about the value of foresight from internal auditors. Historically, however, the profession's greatest changes have been in *response* to evolving stakeholder needs.

Internal auditors have cultivated a long and respected legacy as purveyors of hindsight. Almost all of us are adept at looking at the past year's data and telling management where mistakes were made. But such hindsight has become one of our least valuable skills. Often, our clients are fully aware of past mistakes and likely are looking only for solutions or recommendations for the future.

Meanwhile, with the advent of operational auditing and, ultimately, the introduction of consulting/advice into our portfolio of services, we also became purveyors of insight. Although more valuable than hindsight, it also suffers from limitations in an era when risks are emerging at warp speed. Today's insight may well be tomorrow's hindsight.

There will always be a need for both hindsight and insight. But in an era of near constant change, stakeholders seek to navigate the future more than revisit the past or dwell in the present. That's why we need to concentrate on the risks of tomorrow and provide foresight if we are to not only protect but enhance and create value for our organizations. As purveyors of foresight, our roles as agents of change will enable us to make a difference in the organizations we serve.

The Internal Audit Mindset Focuses on Protecting Value, Not Creating It

Let's begin our look at this issue by examining The IIA's Three Lines Model, published in mid-2020. An update to the widely accepted Three Lines of Defense Model, the Three Lines Model is built on the premise that risk management and sound governance cannot fixate on only defending or protecting value. In my view, this is the chief improvement over the original model.

The introduction to the new Three Lines Model report focuses on four key points that optimize the model for use by any organization:

- Adopting a principles-based approach and adapting the model to suit organizational objectives and circumstances.
- Focusing on the contribution risk management makes to achieving objectives and creating value, as well as to matters of "defense" and protecting value.
- Clearly understanding the roles and responsibilities represented in the model and the relationships among them.
- Implementing measures to ensure activities and objectives are aligned with the prioritized interests of stakeholders.

Additionally, the new model lays out six key principles that help define good governance, the roles of key players in the governance process, the importance and value of independent assurance, and the concept of creating, not just protecting, value. Principle 6 focuses squarely on creating and protecting value:

> All roles working together collectively contribute to the creation and protection of value when they are aligned with each other and with the prioritized interests of stakeholders. Alignment of activities is achieved through communication, cooperation, and collaboration. This ensures the reliability, coherence, and transparency of information needed for risk-based decision-making.

The concept of defining internal audit's value to the organization simply as helping to protect value is outdated. Our stakeholders demand more, and internal auditors must rid themselves of this mindset.

Sometimes, Management Is Happy to Keep Us in Our Safe Place

This may be the most insidious enabler of the profession's resistance to change. Despite being allies, management and internal audit do not always see eye to eye. Disagreements may be easily resolved by a simple rewording in an audit report, or they may be serious enough to impair internal audit's ability to carry out its mission.

This natural tension also can lead to management taking advantage of internal audit's inertia. I have witnessed many cases over my nearly 50 years in the profession where a strong internal audit function is not welcomed by corporate and government executives who would rather keep it as window dressing and not as a window to corporate or government accountability. In 2015, I wrote about this scenario in the context of underpaying the CAE, but it also can apply to allowing internal audit to become entrenched in its comfort zone.

What Can We Do About It?

It is important to step back and look at how the imperative for change fits into the bigger picture for the profession and for overall governance within our organizations. As noted earlier, The IIA's 2030 vision statement set a lofty goal of internal audit being universally recognized as indispensable to effective governance, risk management, and control. I believe that being value creators, not just value protectors, is integral to being universally recognized as indispensable. But bluntly, we've got a long way to go.

The answer to "What can we do about it?" is clear. As a profession, internal audit must:

- Aggressively seek ways to update processes that can keep pace with the speed of risk and abandon those that cannot,
- Truly embrace technology once and for all,
- Alter our mindset to focus on creating value, not just protecting it,
- Recognize our shortcomings and commit to improving them.

Plainly, it is much easier to articulate what must be done than to go out and achieve it. However, as we embark on achieving indispensability, we need to ensure our zeal for change doesn't overtake our common sense. I believe there are five things we must get right as we move forward:

1. **Be a beacon for emerging risks.** This means being a steady and reliable resource of information, assurance, and clear-eyed advice to management and the board on data ethics, AI governance, and

sustainability. Those three issues will have oversized influence on risk and risk management in the coming decade.

2. **Recruit, retrain, and retain game-changing talent.** It is vital that we have the right people to update our processes and help shape our new mindset as agents of change. We must be open to having such talent come from outside internal audit and finance. As late as 2018, about three-quarters of CAEs polled for *The North American Pulse of Internal Audit* report found accounting, finance, or IT-related degrees most desirable. Business, operational, technical, and communications backgrounds lagged well behind.[7] The same survey found that half of CAEs described skills such as data mining/analytics and cybersecurity as only somewhat or not essential skills.

   The dire need for both skillsets could not be clearer today. As demand grows for these talents, it will become increasingly difficult to hire the people we need to transform our processes. CAEs will need to focus on building desired skills within existing staff. Whether hiring from within or outside the organization, building a strategic plan to ensure a steady supply of qualified personnel is critical.

3. **Be champions for strong governance.** By example and through audit work, internal auditors should support sound governance. Principles of sound governance can be found in COSO's internal control and enterprise risk management frameworks, The IIA's Three Lines Model, and The IIA's American Corporate Governance Index's Guiding Principles of Corporate Governance. By helping to ensure our organizations have effective and efficient governance, internal audit adds value and positions itself to effect necessary change.

4. **Innovate for greater efficiency and impact.** We have seen admirable advances in adapting agile work processes pioneered in software development to audit engagement processes. Rather than the traditional linear steps involving planning, fieldwork, review, and reporting, agile internal auditing uses sprints, where those four components are performed simultaneously in a cycle of one to two weeks. The sprints are repeated until the audit is completed.

   Improved collaboration, better transparency, and faster turnaround are the clear benefits cited by proponents, such as Jamie DuBray, KBR's vice president of investor relations and FP&A. While serving as Western Hemisphere Audit Manager at Schlumberger, DuBray helped lead the adoption of agile auditing techniques at the oilfield services company in 2019. It saw average target deliveries for audits cut from 45 days to five days.

This kind of innovation is what will transform internal auditing. From DuBray's perspective, the profession has two options — innovate or become irrelevant. "I don't think we want to be labeled in a way that we are not being relevant. We'll die as a profession if we don't keep up," she said.[8]

5. **Be prolific in telling internal audit's story — how we preserve and CREATE value.** Internal auditors are too often self-effacing and reticent to speak out when it comes to creating awareness about the value we bring to our organizations. This can be partially blamed on the misguided idea that projecting and protecting our reputation for objectivity requires being modest. We can remain objective and independent and still speak boldly about the profession's rightful place as a vital player in risk management and sound governance.

I examine how to achieve these goals in part two, "Enacting the Change," looking specifically at changing our mindset, revolutionizing our processes, leveraging technology, and telling our story.

Next Steps

I debated whether to use a crossroads analogy to hammer home the key message of this chapter. At first, I thought it a bit cliché. Every crisis doesn't have to be a choice of one path or another. But in this case, a slight modification to the crossroads concept offers an important level of clarity and urgency to illustrate the need for change.

Most people envision a crossroads as intersecting roads that offer alternatives on which way to go. But that vision is two-dimensional, like the x- and y-axes on a quadrant graph. The reality is that there is a third dimension.

In this case, the z-axis offers a measure of how steep the journey toward change has become. Until we commit as a profession to innovate our approaches, update stale and slow processes, and embrace technology, the grade will get steeper with each passing day. The other direction on the z-axis provides an easier road. Of course, that road is all downhill, which is a direction we can't afford to go.

I've addressed questions of why where we are today is not good enough and what we can do about it. This leads to a third question: Who will lead us through this change? The answer should be obvious by now — the agents of change among us.

Chapter 2

Responding to Risk in Permacrisis

*There cannot be a crisis next week.
My schedule is already full.*

— Henry A. Kissinger —

As we have noted, emerging risks and the crises they often spawn have become more common occurrences in the 21st century. Fueled by wars, climate change, a global pandemic and technology's unrelenting advancement, the tumultuous initial quarter of the century has introduced a new concept to the lexicon of business and risk management – *Permacrisis*.

Author David Shariatmadari aptly describes permacrisis as:

> *". . . a term that perfectly embodies the dizzying sense of lurching from one unprecedented event to another, as we wonder bleakly what new horrors might be around the corner."*[1]

Shariatmadari's description was part of a blog post noting that *permacrisis* had been named Collins English Dictionary's 2022 word of the year. While the article focused on crises that had befallen the United Kingdom since 2020 — a pandemic and its aftermath, a brutal new war in Europe, an economic crisis that threatened a "material risk to financial stability," and political instability that saw the selection of three prime ministers — a similar list of crises could be describe in other parts of the world. Who could blame Ukrainians battling Russian invaders; residents of the Sudan and elsewhere enduring economic and political upheaval; or residents of Malawi and elsewhere suffering through climate-driven disasters, for believing they lived in a state of constant crisis?

So, how does the specter of constant disruption and calamity fit into our discussion? The answer is fundamental to understanding and embracing the concept of becoming agents of change. The pace of change and disruption is unlikely to slow down. Therefore, we must learn to thrive and embrace a world driven by ambiguity, complexity and even the incomprehensible.

Before we discuss our approach to managing ambiguity, complexity and the incomprehensible and its importance to becoming agents of change, let's examine two strategic frameworks used to make sense of our increasingly erratic world.

VUCA

VUCA, which stands for *volatility, uncertainty, complexity,* and *ambiguity,* was first articulated as a framework in 1987 by the U.S. Army War College to describe a post-Cold War world. By the turn of the millennium, the term had been widely embraced as a strategic leadership model.

The VUCA framework, "provides a lens through which organizations can interpret their challenges and opportunities. It emphasizes strategic foresight, insight, and the behavior of entities within organizations."[2]

VUCA's value to organizations is that it, "underscores the conditions and challenges organizations face when making decisions, planning, managing risks, driving change, and solving problems."[3]

Sound familiar?

The graphic on the following page (see **Exhibit 2-1**) developed by the Harvard Business Review provides additional information on the characteristics, examples, and approaches to each of the VUCA components.

Exhibit 2-1
A Guide to Approaching Events in the Four VUCA Categories

↑ HOW WELL CAN YOU PREDICT THE RESULTS OF YOUR ACTIONS? ↓

Complexity

Characteristics: The situation has many interconnected parts and variables. Some information is available or can be predicted, but the volume or nature of it can be overwhelming to process.

Example: You are doing business in many countries, all with unique regulatory environments, tariffs, and cultural values.

Approach: Restructure, bring on or develop specialists, and build up resources adequate to address the complexity.

Volatility

Characteristics: The challenge is unexpected or unstable and may be of unknown duration, but it's not necessarily hard to understand; knowledge about it is often available.

Example: Prices fluctuate after a natural disaster takes a supplier off-line.

Approach: Build in slack and devote resources to preparedness—for instance, stockpile inventory or overbuy talent. These steps are typically expensive; your investment should match the risk.

Ambiguity

Characteristics: Causal relationships are completely unclear. No precedents exist; you face "unknown unknowns."

Example: You decide to move into immature or emerging markets or to launch products outside your core competencies.

Approach: Experiment. Understanding cause and effect requires generating hypotheses and testing them. Design your experiments so that lessons learned can be broadly applied.

Uncertainty

Characteristics: Despite a lack of other information, the event's basic cause and effect are known. Change is possible but not a given.

Example: A competitor's pending product launch muddies the future of the business and the market.

Approach: Invest in information—collect, interpret, and share it. This works best in conjunction with structural changes, such as adding information analysis networks, that can reduce ongoing uncertainty.

← HOW MUCH DO YOU KNOW ABOUT THE SITUATION? →

Source: Harvard Business Review

BANI

The second framework is BANI, which stands for *brittle, anxious, nonlinear,* and *incomprehensible*. It is a more recent framework whose proponents argue that VUCA is outdated in a world where the default conditions are volatile, uncertain, complex, and ambiguous.

BANI offers a bit of a darker take on understanding and managing conditions in business specifically and the world generally. In a 2020 article, futurist Jamais Cascio argues that BANI, "is a framework to articulate the increasingly commonplace situations in which simple volatility or complexity are insufficient lenses through which to understand what's taking place. Situations in which conditions aren't simply unstable, they're chaotic. In which outcomes aren't simply hard to foresee, they're completely unpredictable. Or, to use the particular language of these frameworks, situations where what happens isn't simply ambiguous, it's incomprehensible."[4]

A deeper dive into understanding BANI will help add context to concepts we touched on in the opening chapter. Let's look at each of the words in the BANI acronym, Cascio's interpretation, and how it relates to agents of change:

Brittle. Cascio argues that systems or organizations that appear strong may actually be brittle. They are not resilient and therefore not well suited to succeeding in an uncertain world. They will shatter when they reach a breaking point. This is why we discussed the importance of tempering in Chapter 1 and how agents of change can support their organizations in a tempering process.

Anxious. Cascio's take on anxiety is particularly interesting. He argues the word, "carries with it a sense of helplessness, a fear that no matter what we do, it will always be the wrong thing. In an Anxious world, every choice appears to be potentially disastrous." As agents of change, we can offer a more positive outlook informed by foresight and understanding.

Nonlinear. Here Cascio argues that, "In a Nonlinear world, cause and effect are seemingly disconnected or disproportionate." Keep in mind the author was writing in the early stages of COVID. The pandemic's shockingly rapid spread and the early struggles to understand and contain it certainly seemed chaotic and disproportionate.

However, the key word in Cascio's writings here is "seemingly". Often what appears as nonlinear, disconnected, or disproportionate may take on a different context in retrospect.

A well-understood theory among risk managers – Black Swans – can help add context to what could appear to be nonlinear. The theory was developed by Nassim Nicholas Taleb, starting in 2001, to explain:

- The disproportionate role of high-profile, hard-to-predict, and rare events that are beyond the realm of normal expectations in history, science, finance, and technology.

- The non-computability of the probability of consequential rare events using scientific methods (owing to the very nature of small probabilities).
- The psychological biases that blind people, both individually and collectively, to uncertainty and to the substantial role of rare events in historical affairs.[5]

Taleb's final point is most relevant here. Humans have become quite adept at rationalizing, particularly in trying to comprehend unexplainable or unanticipated events. Yet, hindsight often can reveal the biases that blinded us to unmanaged risk that led to those events.

The nonlinear effects in BANI also are reminiscent of what is known as "the butterfly effect" in chaos theory. Mathematician and meteorologist Edward Norton Lorenz conjectured the details of a tornado – its exact time of formation, the exact path taken – were influenced by minor perturbations such as a distant butterfly flapping its wings several weeks earlier.

For our purposes, dwelling on the inexactitude of forces that are not well understood or clearly relevant would seem to fly in the face of the definition of risk management – balancing risk and likelihood.

Incomprehensible. To give Cascio his due, he makes an elegant linkage between nonlinear and incomprehensible in his writings:

> "Most importantly, nonlinearity is ubiquitous in biological systems. The growth and collapse of populations, the effectiveness of vaccination, swarm behavior, and, as noted, the spread of pandemics — all of these have a strongly nonlinear aspect. From outside, they're fascinating to watch; from within, they're staggering to experience, as we are now discovering. And sometimes, they're impossible to understand."[6]

Here, Cascio delves into an area that may provide the most value in our discussion, particularly as it addresses an aspect of what is likely to be the greatest influencer of risk and opportunity for the foreseeable future – artificial intelligence.

Cascio argues that as we experience events or decisions that appear to be illogical or senseless, we are left with the troubling condition where, "We try to find answers, but the answers don't make sense." Worse yet, in these cases, more information may not guarantee greater understanding.

"More data — even big data — can be counter-productive, overwhelming our ability to understand the world, making it hard to distinguish noise from signal. Incomprehensibility is, in effect, the end state of 'information overload,'" Cascio writes.

Then his argument touches on what is known as "black box intelligence" in AI.

"Incomprehensibility seems to be intrinsic to the kind of machine learning/artificial intelligence systems we're starting to build. As our AIs become more complicated, learn more, *do* more, the harder it becomes to understand precisely how they make their decisions. Programmers know that there is a web of logic at work but find it difficult to figure out precisely how that web is shaped."

I address AI in depth in Chapter 6, but for now it is important to contemplate the value of accepting what we don't or even can't know.

Embracing Ambiguity, Complexity and the Incomprehensible

Ambiguity, complexity, and the incomprehensible are concepts that will undoubtably play oversized roles in our lives and our work in the future. Tomorrow's leaders will be those who can quickly decipher complex threats and recognize opportunities in crisis. They also will have to possess a level of acceptance or comfort with what is unknowable.

Ambiguity

As agents of change, we should understand that ambiguity refers to the quality of being open to more than one interpretation, meaning, or outcome. It is present in situations where information is incomplete, contradictory, or unclear, and where there are no clear or definite answers.

Historically, forging ahead without clarity has been viewed as dangerous and foolhardy. But the accelerating pace of change will reward those who seek out opportunities amid the chaos, those who are willing to accept short-term failure for long-term success, and those who can make bold decisions driven as much by what they know is certain as what they sense is true.

Complexity

Complexity refers to the state of having multiple interconnected parts, factors, or variables that make understanding, predicting, or managing a situation challenging. It's associated with systems or problems where the interactions and relationships between components create unpredictable behaviors and outcomes.

The characteristics of complexity read much like the components of the BANI framework discussed earlier.

- **Interconnectedness:** Elements within a complex system are interconnected, often in ways that are not immediately apparent.
- **Dynamism:** Complex systems are dynamic and can change and evolve over time.
- **Nonlinearity:** Small changes in one part of the system can lead to disproportionately large impacts elsewhere, making outcomes difficult to predict.
- **Diversity and Variability:** Complex systems often contain a wide variety of elements, each with its own set of behaviors and properties.

Linking Ambiguity and Complexity

While ambiguity and complexity are distinct concepts, they often occur together and can influence each other:

- **Complexity can lead to ambiguity.** The more complex a system or situation, the harder it is to understand clearly, often leading to multiple interpretations and uncertainty.
- **Ambiguity is a component of complexity.** Ambiguity, with its lack of clear, definitive answers, adds to the complexity of situations and decisions.

Why They Matter

Both ambiguity and complexity are inherent in many aspects of modern life, from business and technology to personal relationships and global politics. Understanding and navigating these concepts is crucial for effective decision-making, problem-solving, and strategic planning. They challenge us to think critically, remain adaptable, and continuously learn and evolve.

Agents of Change

Embracing ambiguity and complexity is crucial in both personal growth and professional environments for several compelling reasons:

1. It fosters innovation and creativity. Ambiguity forces individuals and organizations to think outside the box. When the answer isn't clear, people must get creative and explore new ideas. This can lead to breakthrough innovations and solutions that wouldn't have been discovered otherwise.

2. It enhances adaptability. In a world that's constantly changing, the ability to adapt is crucial. Embracing ambiguity helps you become more comfortable with uncertainty and change, making it easier to adjust your strategies and approaches as needed.

3. It improves problem-solving skills. Dealing with complex and ambiguous situations can significantly enhance critical thinking and problem-solving skills. It encourages a deeper analysis and understanding of issues, leading to more thoughtful and comprehensive solutions.

4. It encourages learning and growth. Navigating through ambiguity often requires acquiring new knowledge and skills. It pushes individuals to learn, grow, and expand their horizons, leading to personal and professional development.

5. It builds resilience. Facing and overcoming uncertainty strengthens resilience. It teaches you to cope with and bounce back from challenges, making you better equipped to handle future uncertainties.

6. It enhances decision making. Embracing complexity helps in understanding that problems often have multiple layers and facets. This realization can lead to more nuanced and informed decision-making, considering various perspectives and potential outcomes.

7. It prepares for the future: The future is inherently uncertain. By embracing ambiguity now, you're better prepared to face whatever the future might hold. It helps in building a mindset that is not easily flustered by unforeseen events.

8. It promotes flexibility. In complex situations, rigid thinking can be a significant hindrance. Embracing ambiguity promotes a more flexible approach to thinking and working, allowing for quicker and more effective responses to changing circumstances.

9. It facilitates deeper understanding. Complexity often requires you to look beyond the surface and understand the deeper underlying principles and connections. This can lead to a more profound, holistic understanding of your work and the world around you.

10. It encourages collaboration. Ambiguity often can't be tackled alone. It requires diverse perspectives and expertise. Embracing it encourages teamwork and collaboration, bringing people together to share their insights and find solutions.

While dealing with ambiguity and complexity can be challenging, it's also incredibly rewarding. It pushes individuals and organizations to grow, innovate, and adapt. In a world that's increasingly volatile, uncertain, complex, and ambiguous, the ability to navigate ambiguity is not just an advantage; it's a necessity.

How Incomprehensible Fits In

By definition, incomprehensible is something that cannot be understood. But the key to living and thriving in conditions or crises that appear incomprehensible is understanding that such conditions are rarely static. Very little remains unyieldingly indecipherable. Embracing ambiguity and complexity and the benefits it can create (as outlined above) is what ends the mystery and brings the incomprehensible into the light of reason and understanding.

Chapter 3

Independence Doesn't Imply Isolation

It's not about standing still and becoming safe. If anybody wants to keep creating, they have to be about change.

— Miles Davis —

The imperative for a new and critical step in the evolution of internal audit is evident. The pace of change in technology and disruption demands next-level internal audit services enabled by a specific mindset and skillset. We have discussed the need for internal auditors to be agents of change, but what exactly does that mean?

In the simplest terms, agents of change are individuals or internal audit functions that are catalysts for transformation that creates value within their organizations. We will get into the detail of just what that entails, but for the moment let's first address how today's internal auditors typically approach their jobs. Most internal auditors are conditioned from their first day on the job to pursue a "systematic and disciplined" approach when undertaking internal audit engagements rooted in independence and objectivity. While no longer specifically articulated as part of a definition of internal auditing in the new IIA Standards, those elements remain engrained in practitioners whose careers predate the latest changes to the Standards. However, they must be practiced with the overarching objective of adding value and improving an organization's operations, which are also essential elements of the definition.

Today's internal auditors have, for the most part, evolved to a point where they are comfortable providing both assurance and advisory services. I've written about what I call the "Five A's of Effective Internal Auditing" to convey what internal auditors should strive to accomplish:

Assess risks. Successfully assessing the organization's risks is fundamental to the job of internal auditing. Internal auditors first and foremost must follow the risks. However, we must aim for a broad perspective on how we assess those risks. Beyond identifying those things that threaten to disrupt or impede the organization from achieving its goals, we should assess the adequacy of risk management, organizational governance, and culture. We should understand the board's appetite for risk and evaluate whether executive management is operating within those bounds. To do those things, we must have a keen understanding of the organization's goals and strategies, as well as the industry in which the organization operates.

Align internal audit coverage to focus on the most critical risks. The surest path to failure for internal auditors is paved with personal preferences and priorities. The reason we assess risks is to clearly identify the areas where we need to focus. Fixating on risks with a lower likelihood of materializing, or those whose impact on the organization are likely to be insignificant, will diminish the perceived value of internal audit and ultimately lead to irrelevance. However, internal auditors should never make the mistake of thinking that they must be in lockstep with management in assessing risks or aligning coverage. Having a thorough understanding of goals and strategies, and consistently aligning internal audit with them, offers practitioners the opportunity to provide additional insight and foresight.

Assure management and the board that risks are effectively managed and controls are effectively designed and implemented. This is the legacy service of internal audit. It is essential to protecting value within an organization. Assurance over the effectiveness of financial reporting, compliance, operations, cybersecurity, and other areas affords comfort to management and the board that risks within the organization are effectively managed. Before we can offer such assurance, however, we must have carefully planned, conducted, and reported the results of our engagements. If we identify problems, we should be able to articulate the condition, effect, cause, criteria, and recommendations. Of particular importance is making sure we dig deep enough to expose the root causes of risk management or control failures and weaknesses.

Additionally, assurance over organizational governance and culture takes on more subjective measurements and mandates greater practitioner judgment. Some internal auditors are less comfortable auditing the "soft stuff," but this is increasingly vital to providing effective overall assurance.

Advise management and the board by drawing on our vast expertise. As the risk landscape becomes increasingly complex and fast-paced for most organizations — fed by technology and its disruptive influences — internal audit's advisory services are more important than ever. After all, there is little value in informing stakeholders that mistakes were made when we could have helped to avert the mistakes by advising during design and execution. Assurance is an accurate look in the rearview mirror. However, as every driver knows, accidents are avoided by being aware of your surroundings and — most importantly — looking ahead.

Anticipate tomorrow's risks. The ability to anticipate the organization's needs, as well as its risks, raises internal audit's profile and value. Having a grasp on emerging risks, disruptive technologies, and threats that lie just beyond the horizon helps to make internal audit indispensable. If we are unable to anticipate risks, it is unlikely that we will be able to effectively audit at the speed of risk.

When executed well, the impressive list of services internal audit offers can provide significant value to any organization. But we should take a moment to dive a bit deeper into what internal audit must do to add value and remain relevant.

As noted in the section above on aligning internal audit coverage, "Fixating on risks with a lower likelihood of materializing or risks whose impact on the organization are likely to be insignificant will diminish the perceived value of internal audit, and ultimately lead to irrelevance." In his book, *Ready and Relevant: Prepare to Audit What Matters Most*, author Tim Berichon puts into prescient perspective related statistics on relevance from a recent IIA *Pulse of Internal Audit* report.

"The Pulse reported that only 45% of chief audit executives (CAEs) feel that their internal audit departments are very agile, yet 67% already realize that agility is extremely important in the future. It was surprising that this percentage was not higher, and also surprising that these CAEs feel it is important 'in the future' and not more urgently now...

In response to disruption, the Pulse reported that only 56% of respondents have meaningful collaboration with other lines of defense, 46% have flexible resource planning and allocation, and 36% have flexible talent management. Yet these areas are all very important to help internal audit be more responsive to strategically important matters.

The Pulse also noted that 62% perform work only to the extent of internal capabilities and 65% delay work until they have developed the competencies/skills, or they exclude the area altogether. But what if the topic is very important to the enterprise? It's no wonder internal auditors sometimes feel they are not responsive enough and wonder why they are not more relevant."[1]

Berichon goes on to quote Sir Richard Branson, the English business magnate, investor, author, philanthropist, and founder of Virgin Group, who said, "If someone offers you an amazing opportunity and you're not sure you can do it, say yes — then learn how to do it later."[2]

The bottom line on relevance is that you may perform stellar internal audits that expose control weaknesses or failures and identify root causes, but if they do not focus on areas of importance to the organization, they are not likely to add value. I have always referred to them as the "so what" audits, because management and the board may well say in response to the audit report, "All of that may be true, but it is also not important."

Internal auditors should assess risks, align internal audit coverage to focus on imminent risks, assure management and the board that risks are effectively managed and controls are effectively designed and implemented, advise management and the board by drawing on our vast expertise, and anticipate tomorrow's risk. All that should be accomplished while remaining focused on the organization's goals and strategies. Any practitioner reading the list might say, "Whew, isn't that enough?" In a word, "no."

The challenges today's organizations face are complex, volatile, and often overwhelming. Contributing to overall success requires those in critical roles, such as internal audit, to help the organization in every way possible. For internal audit, that means doing more than providing value. We must also contribute to value creation. We must do more than check to see if all the doors are locked. We must also help the organization decide where new doors should be. If we walk away and things are no better than when we came, we haven't been successful. If our intent is to fix things, and that's all we care about, we are not agents of change — we are agents of correction. We must take the extra step, go the extra mile, and strive to make it *better* than it was before.

It is important to realize that being an agent of change is not a line of service. It is an outcome that is inspired by how we approach our mission. Agents of change are trusted advisors who offer insight and foresight designed not just to fix things that are broken but transform things so they are better. Value that accrues makes the organization more successful.

Independence and Objectivity

Let's next examine how internal audit came to take on the role of an independent and objective assessor of management activities, what that means in a modern organizational context, and how that relates to agents of change.

The concept of independent reporting on management activities began with the creation and growth of corporations in the nineteenth century, when non-management parties were first used to validate management's reports to corporate boards and shareholders. Over time, the task of verifying management reports fell to internal auditors, which is a key evolution from simply being management's monitors of transaction processes.

In his article on internal audit history, *Internal Auditing: History, Evolution, and Prospects*, Sridhar Ramamoorti notes that internal audit started out protecting against payroll fraud and other asset losses, expanded its role to verification of all financial transactions, and "gradually moved from an 'audit for management' emphasis to an 'audit of management' approach (Reeve, 1986)."[3]

He provides additional context in a related endnote, where he addresses the oft-quoted issue of "serving two masters." In brief, there is a predictable conflict between internal audit working for the betterment of the overall organization, which requires the support and cooperation of management, and the unavoidable critique of management performance that comes from internal audit carrying out its duties. Naturally, tensions can rise when internal auditors are expected to carry out their work "fearlessly recognizing their ultimate allegiance to those charged with organizational governance, not management."[4]

This conflict of working operationally for management while serving the interests of the organization overall has long been addressed in The IIA's *International Standards for the Professional Practice of Internal Auditing* (*Standards*). It was not until the issuance of the newest Standards in 2024 that two key components – independence and objectivity – were addressed separately.

The new standard on independence, Standard 7.1 *Organizational Independence*, states in part:

> "The chief audit executive must confirm to the board the organizational independence of the internal audit function at least annually. This includes communicating incidents where independence may have been impaired and the actions or safeguards employed to address the impairment.
>
> The chief audit executive must document in the internal audit charter the reporting relationships and organizational positioning of the internal audit function, as determined by the board (see also Standard 6.2 Internal Audit Charter)."[5]

The intent of the standard is to establish and affirm internal audit's independence and provides internal audit the confidence and ability to review and potentially be critical of the work of management without fear of reprisal.

We have yet to address the role of objectivity in internal audit and how it relates to internal audit independence. It is important not to conflate the two concepts. Indeed, doing so can act as a barrier to serving as agents of change.

Practitioners are quick to embrace and protect internal audit's independence from management, but they must realize as employees of the organization they are not independent of the organizations they serve. Employee or contractor, internal auditors depend on the organization that pays them. Dependence, however, does not preclude objectivity.

Objectivity is an unbiased mental attitude that allows internal auditors to go into an engagement with no preconceived notion of what they are going to find and perform their work without compromise. Standard 2.1 *Individual Objectivity* directs:

> "Internal auditors must maintain professional objectivity when performing all aspects of internal audit services. Professional objectivity requires internal auditors to apply an impartial and unbiased mindset and make judgments based on balanced assessments of all relevant circumstances. Internal auditors must be aware of and manage potential biases." [6]

Objectivity is critically important in that it promotes internal audit as a true broker of assurance. When internal audit reports on the health or weakness of a control or process, its objectivity is at the heart of its credibility.

As the role of internal audit evolved and it was asked to do more for the organization, the likelihood of conflicts that could weaken objectivity increased. Standard 2.2 *Safeguarding Objectivity* directs how internal auditors must, ". . . recognize and avoid or mitigate actual, potential, and perceived impairments to objectivity,"[7] and Standard 2.3 *Disclosing Impairment to Objectivity*, directs how any impairment to objectivity "in fact or appearance" must be disclosed.[8]

Maintaining Independence and Objectivity as an Agent of Change

This examination of independence and objectivity brings us to a point where we now can address whether acting as agents of change — and embracing the mindset of helping the organization create value — is a threat to internal audit independence or objectivity.

Acting for the betterment of the overall organization by assisting or supplementing management's efforts to achieve goals and objectives should never be viewed as a compromise of independence or objectivity. Management is not the adversary. The Standards set out clear directions on how and when CAEs should disclose real or perceived conflicts and how to manage those conflicts when they invariably occur. Internal audit's obligation to the organization's success should be paramount in this discussion. However, that is not always the case.

Too often, protecting internal audit's independence and objectivity is used as a crutch or an excuse to avoid taking on new roles or speaking out, even when doing so would better serve the organization. This is particularly true when it comes to advisory services. Some practitioners avoid giving advice under the guise of avoiding conflicts to independence and objectivity.

However, objectivity doesn't come on the front end of advice. It comes on the back end. The earliest point at which objectivity could be impaired is when internal audit must go back and audit something on which it provided advice. Additionally, the Standards clearly spell out safeguards that can be built into advisory activities to avoid such conflicts.

One of my earliest experiences in an advisory role came when I served as the U.S. Army's director of internal review (audit) at the Pentagon. The U.S. Department of Defense was undertaking a massive project to reengineer travel-expense reimbursement for its more than two million military members and civilian employees around the world. I was asked by the assistant secretary of the Army to serve on a taskforce advising the team designing the new travel reimbursement system. Traditionally, it would have been unheard of for an internal auditor to be in the room when controls were being designed. After all, how could we audit them later? But staying out of the room would mean that the team would be lacking a valuable perspective on control design and implementation. I came away from the experience with a much better appreciation for the value we can add on the front end of important initiatives. Although my role was not critical to the success of the project, I was proud that I had served as an agent of change.

The Three Lines Model

It may be beneficial to look at thought leadership on governance and risk management and the role internal audit plays within the overall organization. The Three Lines Model addresses a key criticism of the old Three Lines of Defense Model - that it was focused on protecting and not creating value.

One significant change was the greater incorporation of the governing body into the model. The Three Lines Model clearly delineates roles and responsibilities of the governing body, as well as executive management and internal audit. Those roles are not limited to risk management, but they also focus on overall governance of the organization.

Chapter 3: Independence Doesn't Imply Isolation

While not a governance model, the increased focus on governance supports both value creation and protection and deals with both the offensive and defensive aspects of managing risk.

The Three Lines Model is built around six key principles:

- **Principle 1:** Governance of an organization requires appropriate structures and processes that enable accountability, action, and assurance.

- **Principle 2:** Governing body roles ensure appropriate structures and processes are in place for effective governance.

- **Principle 3:** Management's responsibility to achieve organizational objectives comprises both first- and second-line roles. First-line roles are most directly aligned with the delivery of products and/or services to clients of the organization and include the roles of support functions. Second-line roles provide assistance with managing risk.

- **Principle 4:** In its third-line role, internal audit provides independent and objective assurance and advice on the adequacy and effectiveness of governance and risk management. It achieves this through the competent application of systematic and disciplined processes, expertise, and insight. It may consider assurance from other internal and external providers.

- **Principle 5:** Internal audit's independence from the responsibilities of management is critical to its objectivity, authority, and credibility.

- **Principle 6:** All roles working collectively contribute to the creation and protection of value when they are aligned with each other and with the prioritized interests of stakeholders.

Most internal auditors should be familiar with these concepts, even if they hadn't before been articulated in a single model or document. Organizations that embrace and embed them in their controls, operations, and cultures will invariably enjoy stronger governance. Adherence should be the goal of all organizations and, once achieved, the concepts should be continually monitored and nurtured.

The model's principles-based approach was designed to provide users greater flexibility. Governing bodies, executive management, and internal audit are not slotted into rigid lines or roles. The "lines" concept was retained in the interest of familiarity. However, they are not intended to denote structural elements but a useful differentiation in roles. The areas of responsibility are generally:

- Accountability by the governing body to stakeholders for oversight.
- Actions (including managing risk) by management to achieve organizational objectives.
- Assurance and advice by an independent internal audit function to provide insight, confidence, and encouragement for continuous improvement.

Some have argued that internal audit should remain well within the "third line" out of an abundance of caution to ensure the independence and objectivity of its staff. However, the refreshed model clearly emphasizes that "independence does not imply isolation." As the update notes, "There must be regular interaction between internal audit and management. There is a need for collaboration and communication across both the first- and second-line roles of management and internal audit."

The point bears repeating: Independence does not imply isolation. This is critical to understanding how internal audit can and should act to create value.

We've addressed how modern internal audit is still evolving into a function that creates value for organizations and how perceived threats to independence and objectivity can hinder providing next-level service. We've also addressed how the Three Lines Model can help dispel a misguided ivory tower mentality about internal audit's independence and objectivity and its role in the organization.

Now for some good news.

How We See Ourselves

A global poll of CAEs conducted by The IIA's Audit Leaders Network (formerly the Audit Executive Center) disclosed that 9 in 10 respondents believe it is appropriate for internal audit functions to act as agents of change. That should be a cause for celebration. A vast majority of CAEs embrace this new mindset that is critical to the profession's continued evolution. However, data from the same survey reflect that the support has not yet translated into meaningful action.

Only 2 in 10 respondents view themselves as agents of change who partner with executive management to drive change that creates value (see **exhibit 3-1**). Nearly as many (15%) say they facilitate change, but it is up to management to drive change. However, nearly half say they use assurance and consulting services to add value and advocate for change. That is encouraging, as this option comes closest to creating value without actually being agents of change.

It is also important to see how others within the organization view internal audit's role as agents of change, as judged from the responding CAEs' perspective. The survey found that 37% of respondents believe management is fully supportive of internal audit driving change within the organization, and 46% said their boards are fully supportive. That may not be resounding support from our stakeholders, but it's a start. We should take this as a challenge to educate our stakeholders about the potential internal audit holds for creating value.

Exhibit 3-1
2 in 10 CAEs Operate as Agents of Change

Response	%
Not sure	1%
None of the above	0%
I partner with executive management to drive change that creates value at every opportunity.	19%
I use both assurance and consulting to enhance value and advocate for change at every opportunity.	46%
I primarily use assurance to protect value and I use consulting to enhance value and advocate for change.	18%
I may facilitate change by identifying deficiencies, but management drives changes.	15%
My role in the organization is to protect value only (not drive change).	1%

Note: Q12: Which one of the following statements most closely reflects your view of yourself as an Agent of Change in your organization? n = 586

We should take heart that half of the CAEs said their internal audit function is viewed as an agent of change within the organization (see **exhibit 3-2**). While not yet an overwhelming mandate, this clearly suggests a strong movement toward an evolution of internal audit as an agent of change.

Key Characteristics of Change Agents

Audit leaders expressed clear views on the attributes they believe are required to be agents of change. Their top choices reflect a strong focus on business skills and knowing and understanding their organizations. About 6 in 10 respondents listed business acumen, understanding organizational objectives, and building relationships as key attributes (see **exhibit 3-3**).

Chapter 3: Independence Doesn't Imply Isolation

Exhibit 3-2
Half of Internal Audit Functions Viewed as Change Agents

Response	Percentage
Not sure	26%
No, not viewed as agent of change	24%
Yes, viewed as agent of change	50%

Note: Q9: Is the internal audit function within your organization viewed as an Agent of Change? n = 606

Exhibit 3-3
Key Attributes of Change Agents

Attribute	Percentage
Tech savvy	9%
Inspirational	9%
Detail-oriented	10%
Intellectual curiosity	19%
Navigates internal politics	29%
Industry knowledge	30%
Courage	33%
Innovative	38%
Dynamic communicator	44%
Strategic	48%
Enterprisewide perspective	53%
Relationship builder	57%
Understands organizational objectives	59%
Business acumen	60%

Note: Q10: What are the most important attributes an internal auditor must demonstrate to be a successful Agent of Change? n = 606

The question is similar to one used to collect data for *Trusted Advisors: Key Attributes of Outstanding Internal Auditors*. The key attributes from the trusted advisors survey were grouped into three broad categories — professional, personal, and relational. The same treatment for data from the agents of change survey sheds additional light on how change agents are viewed by audit leaders. **Exhibit 3-4** categorizes each attribute and adds its ranking from the survey in parenthesis.

Exhibit 3-4
Categories and Rankings of Key Attributes

Professional	Personal	Relational
Business acumen (1)	Innovative (7)	Relationship builder (3)
Understands organizational objectives (2)	Courage (8)	Navigates internal politics (10)
Enterprisewide perspective (4)	Intellectual curiosity (11)	Dynamic communicator (6)
Strategic (5)	Detail-oriented (12)	
Industry knowledge (9)	Inspirational (13)	
Tech savvy (14)		

Four of the top five attributes fall into the professional category, suggesting that respondents see building professional skills as critical to becoming agents of change. Building relationships and being a dynamic communicator from the relational attributes come next. More innate personal attributes, such as being courageous, innovative, and intellectually curious, fall into the bottom half.

We'll examine in more detail how all these attributes translate into individual actions in part three of this book, but it may be valuable to hear now from those who have "walked the talk" as change agents.

Hearing from the Change Agents

Interestingly, the attributes identified in the bottom half of the survey do not align with the views of CAEs who are considered change agent pioneers. These individuals were more likely to list courage and innovation as their top attributes.

Theresa "Terry" Grafenstine, the former longtime inspector general for the U.S. House of Representatives and current EVP, Chief Audit Executive at PenFed federal credit union, identifies courage as her top attribute. "A lot of people associate courage with job functions that put people in potential physical harm, like a police officer or a member of the military, and those obviously require courage," she said. "But as an auditor, having and standing by your convictions, even when it's scary, takes courage."

Courage also is required to challenge conventional thought, and it is critical to sending a clear message to others within the internal audit function about its value, she said. "I would say to CAEs not only is it important for you to go in with that courage and to be able to stand toe to toe, but you need to do that also for your staff. Oftentimes, you're bringing them to these very high-stakes meetings. If they see you kind of buckle . . ."

Brian Foster, former Microsoft general manager over internal audit and current VP and Chief Audit Executive at ServiceNow, sees intellectual curiosity, understanding the details of the business, and being a dynamic communicator as three essential skills for change agents. Two of the three — intellectual curiosity and detail-oriented — ranked near the bottom of the CAE survey.

"The first thing I look for is people who don't just accept the status quo," Foster said. "You know, they love to ask 'why?' It's like the five-year-old who asks why 74 times in a row. But truly, let's challenge why things are done the way they are."

This attribute reflects a curiosity to understand and challenge how things are done. That requires being comfortable in the details, Foster said, but then being able to communicate clearly and concisely to those at the executive level to make a case for change.

For Naohiro Mouri, executive vice president and chief auditor at American International Group Inc., it is a combination of skills that includes subject matter expertise and strong communications. But, he said, it begins with an ability to think differently, which falls into the categories of thinking innovatively and being intellectually curious. Both of those attributes are in the bottom half of the survey results. "I look for the ability to think differently from what we've been doing, being open, being flexible," Mouri said.

Personal Attributes: Nurture or Nature?

The book *Trusted Advisors* describes personal attributes as focusing on "who internal auditors are at the very core of their being. These attributes are ingrained in outstanding internal auditors." But does that preclude that attribute such as being innovative, courageous, intellectually curious, detail-oriented, and inspirational cannot be learned?

Those personal attributes are deeply seated within the best internal auditors, but that doesn't mean each was born with an instinct to innovate, question norms, or battle dragons. Indeed, those are learned attributes nurtured over a lifetime, and each can grow or wane over time.

For example, courage is often discussed as a necessary trait for internal auditors, and over the decades, countless practitioners have put their livelihoods on the line to bring wrongdoing to light. Like many others, I have long believed that Cynthia Cooper, the former vice president of internal audit at WorldCom, is the model of courage in our profession. Her story is well known within internal audit and accounting circles, and she is rightly praised and lauded for having the courage to stand up in the face of enormous pressure and adversity to unearth the $3.8 billion fraud.

In her book, *Extraordinary Circumstances: The Journey of a Corporate Whistleblower*, Cooper counsels internal auditors to "find your courage." But courage doesn't suddenly blossom within an internal auditor simply because there is an expectation or a strong case for it. Cooper's admonition requires practitioners to examine what courage is and under what circumstances their own internal fortitude may be tested.

Courage means more than just speaking out to address a wrongdoing. It also takes courage to admit one's mistakes or step out of our comfort zone. Indeed, stepping out of our comfort zone is critical to becoming an agent of change. The benefits to our internal audit functions, our organizations, and ourselves greatly outweigh the risks.

As internal auditors, we should follow the advice of American businessman Edward Whitacre Jr., who said, "Be willing to step outside your comfort zone once in a while; take the risks in life that seem worth taking. The ride might not be as predictable if you'd just planted your feet and stayed put, but it will be a heck of a lot more interesting."[9]

Trusted Advisors versus Agents of Change

By now you may be asking yourself: What is the difference between a "trusted advisor" and an "agent of change?" The answer may not be evident by merely comparing the definitions I have formulated for the two terms:

> **Trusted advisor:** An internal auditor who builds and sustains trust throughout the organization by leveraging personal, relational, and professional skills and expertise. Trusted advisors are a valued resource in helping organizations enhance risk management and internal controls through assurance and advice.

> **Agents of change:** Internal auditors or internal audit functions that are catalysts for transformation that create value within their organizations.

Simply put, I believe that all agents of change must be trusted advisors, but not all trusted advisors are agents of change. A CEO and others in management should constantly be attuned to the perspectives of trusted advisors. These men and women should have a seat at the table and bring an array of skills and expertise that will help the CEO and others make decisions that benefit the organization. By contrast, agents of change will not only have a seat at the table, but they will also always be armed with transformational ideas. Agents of change won't rest until they have not only offered advice but also had a transformative impact on the organization.

Part Two

Enacting the Change

Chapter 4

Agent Change Thyself

Growth is painful. Change is painful. But nothing is as painful as staying stuck somewhere you don't belong.

— N.R. Narayana Murthy —

We have all heard the expression, "Physician heal thyself." It is an ancient proverb that counsels us to attend to our own defects before those in others.[1] In this chapter, we examine how internal audit practitioners should undertake to improve their own work and the operations of their functions as part of their journeys to becoming agents of change.

In *The Speed of Risk: Lessons Learned on the Audit Trail*, 2nd Edition, I consistently focused on the need for a more continuous approach to risk assessment and auditing at the speed of risk. I made the case that the accelerated pace at which new risks emerge and threaten make annual audit plans "relics of the past" that position internal auditors to address yesterday's challenges instead of today's.

Yet, much of the methodology on which we base our work has not changed much from when I began my own internal audit journey in 1975. Were it not for the use of technology, I would not be able to distinguish a lot of the methodologies from then to now. Given how little we have changed, it is not surprising that the perception of the profession by our stakeholders also has been slow to change. When I consider how we were seen back then — as the "corporate police" constantly churning out "gotcha" reports from cyclical audit plans — I wonder with some dread whether we are still seen that way in some circles.

Whether it is changing outdated processes and methodologies or correcting stakeholder misperceptions, we have much work to do before we can claim to be a profession of change agents. But sometimes the things that appear to hold us back can also hold the answers to our biggest needs.

One of our profession's greatest strengths is the methodical approach we take to our work. Indeed, part of the definition of internal auditing from the 2017 IPPF highlights this strength by describing us as bringing "a systematic, disciplined approach to evaluate and improve the effectiveness of risk management, control, and governance processes." One could make the case that this careful approach to our work also makes us reticent to make changes to our processes. However, nothing in the definition of internal audit precludes innovation, creativity, and imagination.

Appetite for Change

The modern internal auditor's use of statistical analysis, predictive analytics, behavioral psychology, RPA, Agile methodologies, and AI shows that embracing technology and novel approaches strengthens the profession's ability to provide assurance and advice on the effectiveness of risk management, control, and governance processes.

Yet, for too many internal audit functions, the use of more advanced processes is limited. What's more, there seems to be a limited appetite to routinely examine the effectiveness of how we do our work. A sampling of data from various recent reports on the profession reflects the low uptake of technology and slow updating of processes to keep pace with change:

> The majority of internal audit leaders surveyed in AuditBoard's 2024 Focus on the Future are not prioritizing key technology investments in 2024: 66% rated deploying next-generation technologies within internal audit (e.g., AI, RPA, ML) as either "optional" or "not considering," 59% said

the same about implementing or expanding adoption of cloud-based integrated risk management technology.[2]

Protiviti's 2023 Next-Generation Internal Audit Survey offered similar findings and insights, with 52% of CAEs and internal audit directors expressing that "competing priorities, together with a lack of capacity, are barriers or inhibitors to an increased focus on innovation and transformation."[3]

PwC's Global Internal Audit Study 2023: *Seeing through walls to find new horizons*, found that less than half (45%) of internal audit leaders are very confident that internal audit has the talent and skills the function will need in the next three to five years.[4]

Despite those troubling statistics, we should take heart from the profession's history and its consistent ability to pivot to the needs of our organizations. We also should take note of the optimistic tone set by Shannon Urban, VP, CAE at Hasbro and a former IIA North American Board chairman, when discussing the need for innovation within the profession.

"Innovation in internal auditing is both crucial for its growth and necessary in meeting the ever-changing needs of stakeholders," she said. "It is a messy, frustrating, and ongoing program that demands commitment and courage. And it is fun, surprising, and rewarding. All auditors can take a few easy steps to start, or reboot, their journey today. If we want to understand our stakeholders and serve them well in the future, embracing innovation is the only option."[5]

At the same time, we also should heed the warning from the late U.S. President John F. Kennedy, who said, "There are risks and costs to a program of action. But they are far less than the long-range risks and costs of comfortable inaction."[6]

Four Areas in Need of Change

Change is hard. It is fraught with uncertainty. It questions our abilities. It disrupts what we see as an already challenging and complex job. It also is true that, without change, any profession will plateau, eventually decline, and become irrelevant.

Rosabeth Moss Kanter, an Arbuckle Professor at Harvard Business School and director and chair of the Harvard University Advanced Leadership Initiative, offers 10 Reasons Why People Resist Change:[7]

1. **Loss of control.** Our sense of self-determination is often the first thing to go when faced with a potential change coming from someone else.
2. **Excess uncertainty.** People will often prefer to remain mired in misery than to head toward an unknown. As the saying goes, "Better the devil you know than the devil you don't know."
3. **Surprise, surprise! Sudden change is often resisted.** It's always easier to say "no" than to say "yes."
4. **Everything seems different.** People are creatures of habit. Routines become automatic, but change jolts us into consciousness, sometimes in uncomfortable ways.
5. **Loss of face.** When change involves a big shift of strategic direction, the people responsible for the previous direction dread the perception that they must have been wrong.
6. **Concerns about competence.** Change is resisted when it makes people feel stupid. They might express skepticism, but down deep they are worried that their skills will be obsolete.
7. **More work.** Change is indeed more work.
8. **Ripple effects.** Pushback is inevitable. Ripples of change disrupt other departments, important customers, and people well outside the venture.
9. **Past resentments.** The ghosts of the past remain out of sight if everything is in a steady state. But trying something new can reopen old wounds and bring out historic resentments.
10. **Sometimes the threat is real.** Change is resisted because it can hurt. When new technologies displace old ones, jobs can be lost.

While it is important to understand why we resist change, it is not an excuse. The case for change in internal audit is clear and compelling. Many of the issues addressed by Professor Moss Kanter apply to the profession's reluctance to change: loss of control, excess uncertainty, concerns about competence, loss of face, and added work. However, to understand and better serve our stakeholders, as Shannon Urban urges, and to avoid the dangers of "comfortable inaction" that President Kennedy warned about, the profession must address the need for change in four key areas — processes, work products, skillsets, and mindsets.

Processes

It is important to understand that a process is simply a series of steps taken to achieve an end. When we recognize that many of the familiar routines we hold dear are simply steps in a series, we may find it easier to modify them or let them go altogether.

One area where process change has taken hold for the profession is the growing adoption of Agile work methodologies. The Agile process is adapted from Agile software development, which describes the use of specific agile software development methodologies and an associated mindset shift to achieve more value and agility from the internal audit process.[8] *Agile Auditing: Transforming the Internal Audit Process* by Rick A. Wright, Jr., published by the Internal Audit Foundation, provides an excellent in-depth examination of Agile internal auditing. Wright makes the distinction in his book between what he describes as little "a" agile and big "A" agile. The latter addresses the specific Agile process. Little "a" describes process improvement efforts to achieve a more nimble, less wasteful internal auditing process.[9] In my view, it is the little "a" that holds the greatest potential to transform our profession. We explore developing a little "a" agile mindset and the use of big "A" Agile auditing in chapter 5, "Driving Change."

Another insight that supports process change is to separate process from how we define our value. This requires having a clear understanding of what we do.

Work Product

When it comes to how and what we do, the discussion should begin with defining our work product. Here's a shocker: The audit report is not our work product any more than a cereal box is the work product of a cereal maker. The audit report is simply the packaging. Timely, accurate, reliable, and relevant delivery of information to our stakeholders is our product.

Let's take a moment to consider the value of our work product. Organizations are under constant pressure to recognize, leverage, and manage risk to help carry out strategies and achieve goals. Having a clear understanding of the risk landscape and the likelihood and impact of those risks on the organization is imperative. This is how the work we do — providing assurance and advice on the effectiveness of risk management, control, and governance processes — adds value.

However, we must consider that our stakeholders — boards and executive management — must balance a multitude of competing and intertwined interests and priorities. They are constantly barraged with information from myriad sources. If we insist on burying timely, reliable, and relevant information in lengthy reports, we quickly run the risk of becoming *irrelevant*. This insight takes on added significance in the current environment where dynamic risks; environmental, economic and political volatility; and disruptive innovation demand that our stakeholders have the right information at the right time.

Despite that, many practitioners continue to rely on established processes and focus on capturing every trifling detail in their reports. The profession's approach to workpapers is an ideal example of why we must rethink how we develop and deliver our core product. Chapter 5 explores how an agile mindset can enhance the internal audit reporting process. But the timeliness battle is often lost before the reporting process has even begun. One way we impair our performance is by how we document our work.

As a young internal auditor, I took very seriously the painstaking art of documenting the results of my internal audit work in workpapers. I believed that well-organized, comprehensive workpapers were critical to demonstrating the quality of my efforts, and that they were the basis for the audit report I would write at the conclusion of the audit.

I understood that the workpapers needed to include documentation of evidence I examined, and that the evidence needed to be relevant, reliable, sufficient, and useful. I adapted to the culture of the profession of the time. And I came to believe that internal audit workpapers were good, and more workpapers were better.

When I rose to the level of a CAE, my perspective on workpapers changed dramatically. I was determined to achieve greater efficiencies in the department, enhance our capacity to audit more risks, and add value for the organization. I undertook a complete review of our internal audit processes and identified many opportunities for improvement. One area in which we were woefully inefficient was in the conduct of our audits — particularly in the documentation of our audit results in the workpapers.

As I reviewed more of our audits, I came to refer to much of what was included as "happy workpapers." These were packed with evidence that everything was fine; documents that merely confirmed that controls were adequately designed and implemented. When everything an internal auditor encounters during the course of an audit is simply captured and included in the workpapers, they soon can be measured in linear feet.

Standard 14.1

Gathering Information for Analyses and Evaluation identifies the characteristics of the information gathered, which must be relevant; reliable; obtained directly; corroborated; gathered from a system with effective governance, risk management, and control process; and sufficient.[10]

Additionally, Standard 14.6 *Engagement Documentation* requires: "Internal auditors must document information and evidence to support the engagement results. The analyses, evaluations, and supporting information relevant to an engagement must be documented such that an informed, prudent internal auditor, or similarly informed and competent person, could repeat the work and derive the same engagement results."[11]

The IIA offers additional insight when considering sufficiency: "Sufficient information is factual, adequate, and convincing so that a prudent informed person would reach the same conclusion as the auditor."

I am particularly partial to guidance provided in U.S. Government Auditing Standards (the Yellow Book), which offers the following to government auditors on what should be included when documenting evidence in workpapers:

> 8.135.b. "the work performed and evidence obtained to support significant judgments and conclusions, as well as expectations in analytical procedures, including descriptions of transactions and records examined (for example, by listing file numbers, case numbers, or other means of identifying specific documents examined, **though copies of**

documents examined or detailed listings of information from those documents are not required)"[12] (emphasis added).

Every internal audit department should have a system of controls that ensures the quality of audit results. Any that struggle with the timeliness should seriously consider these policies with an eye toward becoming more agile and relevant.

Skillsets

One of the biggest challenges to internal auditing posed by the rapid advance of technology is keeping our skillsets relevant to the needs of our organizations. Auditing cybersecurity comes to mind as one of the most important risks that organizations face in the twenty-first century.

For the past decade, protecting organizations from cyber threats has consistently ranked as a top risk for organizations. Indeed, The IIA's 2024 Risk in Focus report listed cybersecurity as the top risk in every region of the world based on its survey of more than 4,200 internal audit leaders and stakeholders. Yet, the profession continues to struggle with having the right talent on staff to effectively audit this risk.

One of the data points cited earlier paints a gloomy outlook about the profession's ability to grow or adapt its skillsets to quickly adjust in a dynamic risk landscape. PwC's Global Internal Audit Study 2023 found that less than half (45%) of internal audit leaders are very confident that internal audit has the talent and skills the function will need in the next three to five years.[13]

So, how can the profession keep pace? The answer, again, can be provided by the change agents among us. One distinct possibility is that enhanced talent will develop outside the traditional internal audit function.

In late 2019, I offered predictions for the 2020s in a blog post written for Internal Auditor online's *Chambers on the Profession*. Two of those predictions were somewhat prophetic in the context of this discussion.

From "The Road Ahead for Internal Audit: 5 Bold Predictions for the 2020s":

> **The rise of "Uber" auditing.** The "gig economy" — a labor market characterized by the prevalence of short-term contracts or freelance work, as opposed to permanent jobs — will find a natural fit in internal

auditing. The demand for tech-savvy internal audit professionals who can skillfully respond to cyber threats and other technology-related risks already outpaces supply. This will make it increasingly attractive for practitioners with these skills and others to offer their services through short-term, on-demand contracts.

From the chief audit executive's perspective, sourcing strategies will include on-demand professionals. There will soon come a time when it will make more sense to simply call a service or turn to an app that will help locate the needed short-term expert to complete an internal audit engagement or advisory project.

The torch will be passed to a new tech-savvy and tech-fearless generation. *Internal Auditor* magazine recently featured its annual list of Emerging Leaders, and reading the profiles of these young dreamers is like peering through a window into the future.

Their embrace of data analytics, robotics, and blockchain technology is a given. Many not only understand technology but are adept at writing code and designing data-analytics programs. This diverse, multinational group recognizes the value of integrating technology into audit and governance strategies. The most encouraging aspect of this development is that embracing technology is what will best position the next generation of internal auditors to remain trusted advisors.[14]

We all must embrace the zeal displayed by the *Internal Auditor* Emerging Leaders and eagerly build new skillsets that correspond to a constantly changing risk landscape. For the profession overall, it is imperative that we understand that needed skillsets must continue to evolve to match changing risks. To keep pace with changing demands on our skillsets, as well as process and work product, we will need to change our mindset.

Mindset

The common thread that runs through the first three topics — process, work products, and skillsets — is embracing a mindset for change. Beyond thinking about how we audit and what we audit, we must examine why we audit.

The Purpose of Internal Auditing[15] from The IIA's 2024 Global Internal Audit Standards says in part: *Internal auditing strengthens the organization's ability to create, protect, and sustain value by providing the board and management with independent, risk-based, and objective assurance, advice, insight, and foresight.* If our work is indeed to *create*, *protect*, and *sustain*, we also must be prepared to *adapt* to new risk areas and the new demands on our skills that come with them.

Kenneth Chen, current CFO at Aiven, was CAE at Spotify for more than six years. During that time, he built a 25-member team on the premise that helping the organization succeed is fundamental to internal audit's job. Indeed, the function's motto, "Enable growth and protect value by providing insights to anticipate and navigate risks," embraces the change agent attitude. For Spotify, internal audit is the voice in the room supporting growth and innovation while reminding people there is value that must be protected.

"It's about selling the story of the benefit we can bring to the table. It's why we should be at the table and not an afterthought," Chen said in an interview with Deloitte's *Resilient* podcast.[15] "It's why we can help them be successful in their market launch or in their product launch. It's asking those difficult questions that they may not actually have ever thought about and then telling them why it matters to them."

Chen's description of his team's work sounds typical for a progressive internal audit function, but the devil is in the details. For example, his teams are mapped to individual business units to ensure constant communication, which includes quarterly meetings with department heads to update risk assessments. This investment is critical to being viewed as a partner within the organization.

"Spotify is a lot like other tech companies. What happened last quarter is a distant memory. We have to keep updated on strategic projects," he said. "A huge part of the reason we work this way is to integrate ourselves into the business units, understand what they're working on, and help them address risks along the way. If I want to go against the grain on a particular project, I need to provide real-time value that is relevant and to the point."

This approach flips the old internal audit approach of only going to the business unit to "check up" on their work, Chen said. Instead, internal audit at Spotify is driven by helping the company get it right the first time.

Chapter 4: Agent Change Thyself

"I need to be a relevant party," he said. "How do I connect the dots to help you get where you're going? One of my objectives is to provide assurance, but I'm also there to help Spotify succeed."

This mindset is fundamental not just to protecting value but to enhancing and creating value.

Chen's success story at Spotify is built on what he refers to as "selling" the story of internal audit's value to the organization. As he notes, "It's why we should be at the table and not an afterthought." Based on the survey for *Agents of Change*, that message is getting through to many of our stakeholders.

Nearly half (46%) of the CAEs who responded to the survey believe their board/audit committee is fully supportive of internal audit acting as a change agent. If you add those who believe boards are moderately supportive, the figure jumps to 80%. The findings are equally encouraging for executive management, where 76% of responding CAEs believe executive management is fully or moderately supportive (see **exhibit 4-1**).

Exhibit 4-1
Stakeholder Support for Change Agents

Category	The Board/Audit Committee	Executive Management
Not sure	9%	3%
Not supportive	2%	—
Minimally supportive	10%	17%
Moderately supportive	34%	39%
Fully supportive	46%	37%

Note: Q7-8: What is X's position on internal audit driving change within your organization? n = 606

So, what is holding us back? The survey provides some insights into that question. While more than three-quarters of CAEs believe they have moderate to full support to act as value creators within their organizations, only half believe their internal audit functions are viewed as agents of change (see **exhibit 4-2**).

Exhibit 4-2
Few Internal Audit Functions Viewed as Agents of Change

Response	Percentage
Not sure	26%
No, not viewed as agent of change	24%
Yes, viewed as agent of change	50%

Note: Q9: Is the internal audit function within your organization viewed as an Agent of Change? n = 606

To close the gap, we must begin by forging a culture of change within internal audit that embraces the change-agent mindset.

Developing a Culture of Change

Managing and swaying culture within an organization is challenging. There are many influencing factors, internally and externally. Tone at the top — the messages both overt and covert put out by leaders — is the most talked about, but there are other dimensions. The profession's recent foray into auditing culture provides insight to help us look at culture within our internal audit functions. We'll delve more into culture and its impacts on change in the next chapter.

One clear and early lesson on auditing culture is understanding that what is done is more important than what is said. In *The Speed of Risk*, I devoted a chapter to auditing culture. One key takeaway was that understanding what culture is — and isn't — is critical.

> "One definition describes culture as the 'moral fabric' of the organization. Another describes it as 'the self-sustaining pattern of behavior that

determines how things are done.' I tend to prefer a much simpler definition: Culture is 'how we do things around here.'

This short phrase packs a big punch as much for what it says as what it doesn't say. It's important to understand that culture is defined by the actual day-to-day operations, interactions, and influences within an organization, not what a mission statement, CEO speech, or employee policy manual says it is. Culture is not what is said; it's what is done."

This is particularly apropos when discussing culture within an internal audit department. For years we have been talking about becoming more agile and flexible, improving communications with stakeholders, embracing technology, and updating processes. Yet, for all the talk, actions and real change have been slow to follow.

Too many internal audit functions are content to operate in a safe and familiar environment. But we must recognize that the purpose of an audit engagement is not to simply point out errors, or cause an impact and then make recommendations on how to not do it again. That has limited value. While it protects value, it rarely enhances or adds value.

Truly innovative and dynamic audit departments are constantly reinventing the way they do things. CAEs must set a tone at the top that embraces and nurtures innovation and change. That starts with internal audit's own strategic plan, which must be forward-looking and provide a roadmap for needed change within internal audit.

I have long asserted that the biggest strategic risk for internal audit functions, and even the profession itself, is complacency. From my experience, success more often begets complacency than more success. The CAE change agents in our profession are restless visionaries who strive for their departments to drive needed change in the organization. They work constantly to improve and enhance the internal audit function and are never content to "do things the way they have always been done."

These CAEs drive their internal audit functions to be agile, flexible, and willing to embrace change — subtle or radical — depending on the risks and the needs of the organization. If you are not willing to change your approaches and processes, it's unlikely you will ever be an agent of change. The agile mindset says, "I'm going to do what I need to do to deliver answers in time to make a difference."

Chapter 5

Driving Change

*Life is either a daring adventure or nothing.
To keep our faces toward change and behave like free
spirits in the presence of fate is strength undefeatable.*

— Helen Keller —

The word *agility* gets used a lot these days. In recent years, it has been infused into the mainstream vocabulary of the internal audit profession. Books and articles abound on "agile auditing." It would be difficult to find an internal audit conference where at least one presenter isn't speaking on agile auditing. So why has agility become such an imperative? I believe it's because of where we find ourselves and where we as a profession aspire to go. I believe that for agents of change, disruption, change, and agility are inextricably linked.

In this chapter, I delve into the features and benefits of Agile auditing and how it can contribute to meaningful change. However, I'll also address how the need and even genuine desire for change sometimes must overcome yet another significant hurdle to find success — culture.

A Case Study in Agility

As I prepared to write this chapter, I was struck by the fact that I have actually been espousing agility for our profession for more than 25 years. Agility became an imperative for the first major audit leadership assignment in my career as director of the U.S. Army's Worldwide Internal Review Program.

In the early 1990s, the long-simmering Cold War between the west and former Soviet-bloc countries suddenly ended. In the United States, the words "peace dividend" quickly emerged, signaling a strong desire by taxpayers and political leaders to reduce the heavy burden of defense expenditures that had been perceived as necessary for decades. As an internal auditor in the U.S. Army, I began to quickly see the consequences of reduced budgets on military operations and readiness that were often the focus of our audit plans. It didn't take long before the spending cuts began to directly impact the budgets of our internal audit departments.

It was during this period of disruptive budget reductions that I assumed the role as the Army's director of internal review based at the Pentagon. While I was honored to take on such an important post, I felt a little like the captain of the Titanic right after it hit the iceberg. In the five years before then, budgets at internal review offices worldwide had reduced the total size of staff from 2,100 to 1,400. The Army overall hadn't shrunk by one-third, yet internal audit resources were frequent targets. Some departments were reduced by 75%, and others eliminated altogether.

At the encouragement of Army leadership, I undertook an extensive study to understand better why internal audit's stakeholders were pulling the plug on us. I traveled around the world, visiting about two dozen offices. At each location, I would sit down with senior military executives to understand where internal audit was falling short and why it was seen as so expendable. The insights I gained from those conversations have stuck with me to this day.

I learned that internal audit was being drastically reduced because its stakeholders didn't feel we added value at a time when they had to make tough budget decisions. Specifically:

- Internal audit wasn't focused on the real risks its organization faced.

- Internal audit's reports often didn't offer meaningful solutions.
- Internal audits took too long and frequently delivered information too late.
- Internal audit reports were often long-winded and difficult for busy leaders to digest.

As I chronicled in *The Speed of Risk*, the feedback was eye-opening:

> "You know, those guys come in and tell me what I already know," some of them said. Others responded, "They tell me things are broken, but I already know they are broken. I need somebody who can tell me how to fix them." Conversely, more than once I heard this: "Sometimes I only need to know 'what time it is,' but the internal review guys insist on giving me voluminous reports that tell me 'how to build the watch.'"[1]

The outcome of my study was a call to action for our worldwide team. We knew we needed to move swiftly and decisively to address the weaknesses exposed in our approach. In short, we had to be willing to change our audit processes so that we would become perpetually agile in the way we delivered our services.

Faced with the loss of stakeholder confidence and other daunting challenges, we embraced an agile mindset and deployed the little "a" agile internal auditing process. We transformed ourselves to achieve a strategic vision of being *"the premiere source of information for the Army's decision-makers."*

Our objectives were to execute our mission smarter, faster, and with more impactful results. We developed strategies around people, processes, and technology. The key features of our "reengineered" approach included:

- Deploying a staff sourcing strategy that included full-time, contract, and guest auditors.
- Transforming the audit planning process so that it centered on crisp, clear, and concise objectives as opposed to those that were broad and open-ended.
- Adopting audit methodologies that leveraged state-of-the-art technologies of the time and deemphasized extensive unnecessary documentation and review.

- Streamlining audit reporting processes focused on timely delivery of the final audit report.

Our quest for greater agility to serve the needs of our customers delivered remarkable results. In less than four years, we reduced the average cycle time for internal audit engagements Army-wide from 56 days to only 14. We enhanced our return on investment — in this case, the cost of operations versus identified, agreed-to savings. As we measured it, our ROI jumped from 3-to-1 to an astounding 24-to-1.

I view agile auditing much like I do enterprise risk management. It's not as critical that you embrace a formal framework or structured approach, such as "Agile" auditing. It's more important that you leverage an agile mindset to constantly strive for efficiency and be able to pivot swiftly in executing the internal audit mission. Our journey was the right one for us under the circumstances, but today many internal audit functions are embracing big "A" Agile internal auditing. And the results can be quite impressive.

Agile Auditing

As we discuss throughout this book, the twenty-first century has brought new challenges and opportunities for the internal audit profession. The speed of risk has increased exponentially, and traditional internal audit methodologies have struggled to enable the profession to keep pace. The emergence of Agile auditing has offered promise to the profession. A survey of more than 1,000 internal auditors by software provider AuditBoard revealed that 82% believe Agile auditing, "has the potential to add more value to their work compared to the traditional project approach."[2]

Aaron Wright, AuditBoard director of product solutions, helped define Agile auditing in a recent whitepaper:

> Agile is a term that's used to describe a set of principles and methodologies that were initially formed for use in software development and popularized by the Agile Manifesto for Software Development in 2001. This included four values below and 12 principles that focus on delivering value. The values shown here recognize that, while all elements are needed, those in **bold** should take precedence over those *italicized*.

1. **Individuals and interactions** over *processes and tools.*
2. **Working software** over *comprehensive documentation.*
3. **Customer collaboration** over *contract negotiation.*
4. **Responding to change** over *following a plan.*

> Agile allows project teams to focus on delivering value, and acknowledges that the traditional "heavy" project management methodologies (namely, Waterfall) follow a linear process that often slows teams down. "Agile" in and of itself is not a process framework, but rather a general term describing a collection of "light" project management frameworks — Scrum and Kanban being the most popular.[3]

The concept of developing a customized "Agile Manifesto" for those internal audit departments that seek to adopt Agile auditing is a great idea. Deloitte encourages creation of a manifesto that is aspirational as well as practical. As one of the first efforts in adopting the methodology, the exercise of developing the manifesto may be more valuable than the manifesto itself."[4]

The firm offers an "Internal Audit Agile Manifesto" for consideration by those contemplating adoption of the methodology. It includes nine elements:

1. Outcome-driven | Value-driven
2. Just-in-time | Proactive approach to the "right projects at the right depth/focus"
3. One size does not fit all — customized project focused on value and risk
4. Collaborative approach — take the journey with our clients
5. Mix it up a little bit, break some eggs — challenge "That's the way we've always done it."
6. Decisioning "as you go" with transparency and alignment
7. Continuous communication with all stakeholders
8. Be quick and iterative versus confined to a plan
9. Impact over thoroughness — "good enough" (80/20 rule)[5] As Deloitte notes, the manifesto should not be set in stone. Those deploying Agile

auditing should add, delete, or modify elements of their manifesto as they become more experienced with it.[6]

However, for me, Toby DeRoche, author of *Agile Audit Transformation and Beyond*, offers the most compelling reason for the value of Agile auditing both to internal audit and the organization.

> "Agile auditing focuses on the risks that matter most to management right now."[6]

Features of Agile Auditing

DeRoche's book provides a wealth of material to guide internal auditors on the Agile auditing journey. Two of the more useful are a set of principles and a list of getting-started tips:

Agile Audit Principles

1. Our highest priority is to support management's objectives by auditing critical and emerging risks.
2. Welcome changing requirements, even while executing the audit plan. Agile auditing accepts change for the best interest of the organization.
3. Deliver audit insights frequently, with real-time results during an audit and at least quarterly to the audit committee, with a preference for a shorter timescale.
4. Business managers and auditors must work together daily throughout the project.
5. Build audits around motivated individuals. Give them the environment and support they need and trust them to get the job done.
6. The most efficient and effective method of conveying information to management and the audit team is face-to-face conversation.
7. Providing insight into the risk and control environment with senior leadership is the final measure of progress.
8. Agile auditing promotes a timely understanding of risk to operations. The first, second, and third lines of defense should maintain open communication and sharing of results.

9. Continuous attention to technical and soft skills enhances audit agility.
10. Simplicity—gaining insights into a risk and control environment without expanding the scope—is essential.
11. The best assessments, audits, and insights gained emerge from self-managing teams.
12. At regular intervals, the team reflects on becoming more effective, then trains and adjusts its processes accordingly.[7]

Seven Steps to Prepare for Agile Transformation

1. Shift mindset to embrace change as the new constant
2. Designate agile team members—with emphasis on project management skills
3. Evaluate current tools for gaps to ensure technology enables "agile" auditing approach
4. Prepare your team with specific agile policies & procedures and training
5. Implement modern technologies to improve audit efficiencies
6. Tie audits to business priorities to audit the right risks at the right time
7. Be agile with your agile transformation[8]

The IIA does not yet provide authoritative guidance that prescribes required features of Agile auditing. Instead, as noted earlier, the practice to date subscribes broadly to the Agile Manifesto for Software Development. However, there are common features that have emerged in Agile auditing. Rick Wright provides an overview in his book *Agile Auditing: Transforming the Internal Audit Process*. Among the key beneficial elements Wright describes are:

> **Value over objectives.** Agile IA (internal audit) engagements define the value to be sought from the engagement up front. This helps ensure the focus throughout the audit engagement is on the goal of producing value for the organization by aligning audit deliverables with strategies and objectives of the organization.

Client involvement. In some iterations of Agile IA, audit clients are invited to be an integral part of the engagement project team. This greatly enhances communication between parties because there is more frequent audit client interaction throughout the engagement lifecycle. Complex projects can benefit tremendously from the subject matter expertise the audit client may offer the project team. This feature is incorporated by design into mature Agile IA implementations.

Time-boxed discipline. Time boxes are fixed length work cycles usually measured in weeks. Because Agile IA engagements are completed in a series of incremental workflows that are time boxed, there is built-in discipline for planning and completing audit tasks on time. This greatly reduces the risk of audit engagement budget overruns and enhances the audit team focus.

Timely insights and risk responses. When audit clients are made a part of the engagement team, they are walking the audit journey side by side with the audit team as work is completed. This means audit clients are also getting real-time feedback on audit results and corresponding insights. Rather than audit insights being delayed while results are validated (as in traditional waterfall audits), audit clients can begin formulating responses to risk right away.

Point-of-view insights vs. fact-focused findings. Agile IA values the process of learning throughout the engagement. This allows for the audit team to develop points of view about the audit subject that go beyond mere findings of fact.

Fewer disagreements on results between audit team and audit client. Because audit clients are deeply involved as an Agile IA engagement progresses, there are opportunities for audit results to be discussed, mutually vetted, and agreed upon concurrently with the audit team. This feature of Agile IA can greatly reduce the potential for disagreements in audit conclusions and increases the likelihood that audit clients will fully embrace audit results and take stronger ownership positions toward responses.

Documentation rationalization. A key principle of Agile software development advocates for simplicity. This is a powerful idea for making the audit process more efficient. Workpaper documentation is a potential area of significant waste in traditional waterfall audit methodology. The amount of extraneous documentation that has found a mainstream footing in traditional audit engagements can be overwhelming and frustrating to audit staff, and often adds little or no incremental value. Agile IA challenges a common myth that more is better in regard to documentation, as well as other areas of waste in the audit cycle.[9]

The Benefits of Agile Auditing

The benefits of Agile auditing are quickly apparent, even in the preceding basic examination of its features. Chief among them are speed and responsiveness. As traditional waterfall methodologies are shelved for Agile methodologies, internal audit teams are discovering that many of the obstacles to auditing at the speed of risk become less daunting.

Agile auditing has gained traction in recent years. Books, articles, and training are readily available. Yet, its proponents would argue that the rate of adoption has been too slow. Part of that is caused by the general resistance to change, as we've already examined. Add to that, internal auditors are, by nature, risk averse. But culture within an organization can be one of the biggest obstacles to genuine change.

As agents of change looking to drive change, we must recognize the significant role of culture within organizations and become skilled at overcoming culture-driven resistance to change.

Understanding the Power of Culture

Much has been written about the influence of bad or toxic culture contributing to high-profile business scandals. Sadly, the list of persons associated with corporate scandals this century reads like a Who's Who of one-time business darlings—Ken Lay at Enron, Bernie Ebbers at WorldCom, Travis Kalanik at Uber, Elizabeth Holmes at Theranos, Sam Bankman-Fried at FTX to name a few. While the circumstances surrounding each scandal are varied, corporate culture eventually emerged as a significant contributor in each case.

In the past decade, the value of auditing culture to identify potential wrongdoing has become clearly apparent. This realization among boards, shareholders, and other stakeholders was long overdue. To be fair, part of the fault lies with internal audit's reluctance to take on culture audits, and I said as much in Chapter 13 of *Speed of Risk*:

"When I launched my internal audit career, the idea of auditing the 'softer' side of an organization's culture was anathema to the profession. Back in the day, it was believed internal audit should focus on hard controls, such as codes of conduct or human resources policies. Evaluating concepts as intangible as trust, ethics, competence, and leadership styles was something for psychologists and pop-culture gurus to worry about. In retrospect, a lot of heartache and failure across a multitude of organizations might have been prevented had internal audit taken on the full spectrum of culture 40 years ago. As it is, the concept is only now gaining broader acceptance among internal auditors and their stakeholders. All I can say to that is, it's about time!

Some longtime practitioners might say that auditing corporate culture is nothing new. After all, we have been talking about tone at the top for decades. But that doesn't quite capture the significant value that a thorough and ongoing assessment of culture can do for preserving an organization's ethical well-being. Just as important, understanding and monitoring culture can protect an organization from misguided or even toxic influences that might serve short-term goals but threaten the organization's long-term success and even survival. Others question whether internal auditors can develop the skillsets to successfully audit corporate culture, which I believe is possible. The profession has undergone significant changes on multiple occasions through the years, and each time practitioners have pivoted successfully to meet stakeholder needs. When it comes to assessing corporate culture, I believe internal auditors will answer the call to action again.

Even if we set aside the question of whether internal auditors have the skills and mandate to fully audit culture, there are practical concerns that will inexorably push the profession in that direction. The speed at which risk related to culture has been exposed is an enormous threat to organizational well-being. There have been too many big companies and organizations getting into trouble in recent years over actions that clearly had cultural components, from FIFA and Volkswagen to Wells Fargo and Uber. Even the most reluctant among us should acknowledge that culture is a big risk, and risk must always be an area of focus for us."

In the five years since I wrote those words, the influence of culture as a pivotal factor in corporate governance has only become more widely understood and accepted. Yet, acknowledging the influence of culture, and doing something to proactively monitor and manage it are two different issues.

A 2022 report on corporate culture found that while 92% of 1,348 North American executives surveyed said they understood improving culture would increase organizational value, a mere 16% believed their organization's culture was where it needed to be.[10] Further confirmation of the struggle to manage culture was demonstrated in a culture survey and report in which I teamed up with Cynthia Cooper.

Two datapoints from AuditBoard's 2023 *Organizational Culture and Ethics Report: Understanding Culture as Culprit, Catalyst, and 21st-Century Differentiator*[11] show that there remains much work to be done on culture:

- While, 68% of 350 internal audit leaders surveyed believe executive behavior is a top indicator of culture risk,
- 37% of their organizations undertake no formal assessment of culture.

For our purposes, the preceding discussion lays the groundwork for understanding how culture within an organization can impact our efforts to become agents of change.

Culture as an Impediment to Change

In *Speed of Risk*, I examined various definitions of culture. I found the simplest definition to be the best; "culture is how things are done around here." Understanding how this simple truism influences change within an organization is vital. By definition, agents of change are drivers of innovation and growth, but rigid, risk-averse and/or toxic corporate cultures present significant barriers to accomplishing any change, much less the meaningful and transformative change that we strive for.

Indeed, being an agent of change in an entrenched and resistant culture is like trying to mine through granite. Therefore, operating with a resistant culture requires agents of change to consider the limits of what they can accomplish.

Under the best of circumstances, cultural change is difficult and gradual. In more challenging circumstances, it can be downright dangerous. Agents of change must weigh whether their efforts to effect positive change must first overcome a resistant culture. They may conclude that such efforts would prove frustrating at best and fruitless at worst.

Culture as an Enabler of Change

In contrast, organizations that have a positive culture provide a welcome haven for agents of change. These organizations understand the value of ethics; conformance to laws, regulations, and organizational policies; and the equal and judicious application of rules. This is a solid foundation on which agents of change can build their careers and become true catalysts of change.

Examining some characteristics common to organizations with strong and positive corporate cultures helps explain why such places can be fertile breeding grounds for agents of change:

- Employees prefer to work for companies whose corporate culture aligns with their own beliefs.
- Positive corporate culture makes for happier and more effective employees.
- Well-defined cultures attract like-minded professionals.
- Strong corporate cultures encourage better communication among employees, which in turn provides an advantage over the competition.
- Employees who are valued and empowered within a strong culture feel they have more control over their jobs. Even remote workers often feel more valued and achieve higher levels of performance.
- Strong cultures encourage employees to grow within their roles.
- Merit-based promotions and training motivate employees and add to an overall positive corporate culture.[12]

It's not hard to connect the dots between this list of characteristics of a positive corporate culture and the ideal environment for those who wish to innovate and drive for positive change.

Chapter 6

Leveraging Enabling Technology

When in doubt, choose change.

— Lily Leung —

As we have explored, internal auditors must have an agile mindset to be effective agents of change. That agile mindset must drive innovation, either through informal or formal transformation of audit processes. But transformation of manual processes alone rarely produces the impact that change agents must deliver. To be powerful change agents, internal auditors must also be tech-savvy and tech-fearless, and leveraging IT starts with the use of enabling technology in the internal audit function itself.

In my 12 years as president and CEO of The IIA, I witnessed firsthand how technology evolved to better serve those in our profession who strive to be agents of change. Advancements in data analytics, audit automation software, RPA, and AI technology, as well as the industry's embrace of Agile auditing methodologies and principles, have enabled audit teams to perform their jobs more efficiently, accurately, and strategically. Frankly, innovation has become essential to helping internal auditors effectively provide the assurance and advisory services required of their roles.

This is especially valuable because events such as the COVID-19 crisis, the ever-growing threats of cyber risk, social unrest, and economic uncertainty have placed increased pressure on internal audit functions to become more dynamic and agile to help their organizations manage these and other risks. Periods of dynamic risk have brought with them challenges, including enabling a distributed workforce, helping organizations identify and address new and emerging risks, and supporting efforts to meet shifting compliance requirements.

The 2023 KPMG Audit Committee Insights[1] survey provides additional affirmation of the need for agents of change who embrace technology. Not only do 55% of the 768 survey respondents think internal audit can increase its value by focusing more on critical enterprise risks, 47% say evolving its data/technology-related skills and capabilities would do so, as well (see **exhibit 6-1**).

Exhibit 6-1
Stakeholder Views on Expanding Internal Audit's Value

On average, CAEs provide assurance on 4 or 5 of the risks listed below — most commonly cybersecurity, third party, business continuity/crisis management, and data governance.

Q7. Which of the following risks do you provide or anticipate providing assurance on in 2020 and/or 2021? (Multi-Select)

Risk	%
Cybersecurity	84%
Third party	71%
Business continuity & crisis management	71%
Data governance	66%
Organizational governance	45%
Board information	24%
Talent management	23%
Culture	21%
Sustainability	19%
Disruptive innovation	14%
Economic & political volatility	11%
None of the above	3%

Yet, technological improvements alone won't help internal audit effectively adapt to new conditions and overcome obstacles; it takes internal auditors with a change-agent mindset to advocate for adoption of technology that can help them drive valuable outcomes. There are many internal audit teams that have dramatically enhanced performance using technology. A good example is United Bankshares (UBSI), a $19.7 billion regional bank holding company with dual headquarters in Washington, DC, and Charleston, West Virginia. From 2011 to 2017, the company completed four significant acquisitions that more than doubled its asset size. Tasked with rapidly scaling their audit program to cover new areas, aligning with new regulatory requirements and audit quality standards, and keeping pace with the company's growth, UBSI's senior internal audit manager and her internal audit managers realized it was time to seek a better organized, user-friendly software platform for their 26-member team.

UBSI's internal audit leadership successfully advocated for making a change that streamlined formal audit procedures through automation, optimized coordination between internal audit and its stakeholders, and scaled their Sarbanes-Oxley 404 control suite. That freed up time and resources to address new risk areas associated with the company's growth while reducing internal audit's budget by 35% a year. Those efficiencies and cost savings were achieved by switching from an older tool to a flexible, cloud-based solution called AuditBoard that could grow with their audit program.

UBSI nicely illustrates audit leaders who embrace a change-agent mindset by leveraging technology to create value for their business. Yet, while UBSI's success story is inspiring, it is a disturbingly rare scenario among internal audit departments.

In this chapter, I examine internal audit's long-simmering love/hate relationship with technology, including diving into the history of technology adoption. I describe critical areas where I believe technology is crucial for building a change-enabling foundation and discuss what to look for in first-rate solutions that empower auditors to be agents of change.

Staying the Course: Is It Worth It?

Internal audit functions must keep pace with the speed of the organizations they serve. Yet, research suggests that internal audit lags other departments when it comes to adopting automation software to streamline their day-to-day audit activities, such as planning, fieldwork, issue management, and reporting to the audit committee and board. A recent IIA survey of more than 500 U.S. and Canadian internal audit leaders found that, while more than a third of respondents reported increased use of emerging technologies such as data analytics and Agile auditing techniques, a mere 12% reported increased investment in automation software.[2]

Yet, in less than a generation, automation software has become synonymous with doing business. The list of examples is long and familiar: Netsuite (accounting); Workday and ADP (human resources and payroll); Salesforce (sales); Atlassian (engineering and project management); Zendesk (customer service); and Hub-spot and Marketo (marketing). These cloud-based solutions have dominated their respective industries not only because they are effective collaboration platforms, but because they are specifically designed to help create efficiencies through organization and automation of day-to-day department processes.

In contrast, the go-to "solution" for far too many audit functions remains spread- sheets, email, shared drives, and homegrown tools. The greatest drawback to this approach is the large amount of administrative work that auditors must perform to manage their audit projects. Valuable time is lost to manual, repetitive activities and reconciling version-control issues, not to mention that a decentralized control environment often leads to a lack of visibility, inefficiencies, and redundancies in activities among audit, risk, and compliance groups.

One rarely discussed reason why the industry has been slow to adopt automation software is that purpose-built audit automation technology didn't begin hitting its stride until recent years. Prior to that, traditional governance, risk, and compliance solutions were the primary options available to audit departments. While those solutions were designed for use by the C-suite with optimized dashboards and reports, they were not built to automate audit lifecycle processes or improve on-the-job collaboration for auditors and their stakeholders. In recent years, a new breed of solutions has begun to proliferate with deeper domain expertise, focus on user experience, and higher engagement and collaboration by audit users and their stakeholders. They are designed to automate the administrative activities essential to the auditor's day-to-day work by centralizing all internal audit data in one reliable location that acts as the single "source of truth." The capabilities of these new solutions far exceed those of spreadsheets and the older technologies, with departments that successfully implement them reporting time savings of 33% to 50% on administrative audit work performed during testing and documentation.[3]

Using Technology to Reengineer Internal Audit Processes

In *The Speed of Risk*, I made the case that excessive cycle times lead to outdated results, which diminish internal audit's value and lead to stakeholder dissatisfaction. I identified five internal audit processes as key candidates for reengineering: risk assessments, audit planning, documentation and review, reporting, and monitoring, and follow-up.

When managed manually, these processes are neither efficient nor cost-effective. Yet, the majority of a staff auditor's workload at any given time consists of some combination of these activities. It stands to reason that strategies to improve these activities through automation software and emerging technologies such as RPA and AI are *capacity multipliers*. In other words, the hours saved multiply an auditor's capacity to take on new projects. The extent to which auditors can employ technology to eliminate administrative activities and shorten the audit lifecycle frees them to work on projects of greater value to the business.

Let's look deeper into emerging technologies to understand how they can create greater efficiency, effectiveness, and value-add capacity for internal audit and the business.

Audit Management Software Helps Add Value

Audit management solutions, also known as audit automation solutions, help streamline workflows. At its core, cloud-based audit management software is a true digital system of record that unifies audit data in one place. Having a single, reliable source of data is foundational to begin automating processes that save valuable resource hours. I will explore this from the perspective of the audit processes that I believe are key candidates for reengineering:

> **Risk assessment.** PwC's recent State of the Internal Audit Profession study reveals that today's audit, risk, and compliance executives almost universally agree that annual plans and annual assessments are antiquated.[4] The most effective risk assessments are the ones that are continuous in nature. In an ever-evolving risk landscape, more frequent risk assessments help organizations stay on top of key risks,

especially during critical times of crisis, such as the COVID-19 pandemic, when audit leaders reported they were performing quarterly and even monthly risk assessments. Audit management software helps automate the distribution and aggregation of risk surveys, as well as the scoring process, saving considerable time for auditors and making it easier to deploy risk assessments more frequently. Software with suitable underlying architecture will link real-time risk data collected from risk assessments to controls and action plans throughout the platform.

Audit planning. In a dynamic risk environment, audit leaders are more frequently changing their audit plans throughout the year. The key features of an efficient and effective engagement-planning process include:

- Ensuring that risk assessment is the primary basis for determining objectives, scope, and specific tests.
- Using a sound and consistent methodology.
- Leveraging expertise from subject matter experts.
- Incorporating advice from management and operating personnel.
- Designing each engagement for efficiency, keeping the budget in mind.

Audit management software can facilitate the planning process by allowing audit teams to manage and collaborate on their audit plans and allocate resources in one place, driven by real-time risk assessment data that live within the same platform. The centralized nature of audit management software can provide auditors with flexibility to make changes to their audit plan quickly and to see those changes updated in real time. As audits progress, managers have real-time visibility into the status of their audit plan and can see how it tracks against department timelines and goals.

Documentation and review. In a manual environment, evidence management entails hours of reaching out to business owners and following up over email. A best practice is for these processes to follow a sound and documented methodology, rather than exist scattered across computers, emails, and differing versions. Audit management software stores all relevant audit documentation in one place, as well as automating its collection, updating, and reviewing processes, saving auditors time and effort.

Reporting. Audit management software is inherently equipped to help auditors provide stakeholders with more insights through real-time dashboards and reporting. With all audit data in one place, internal auditors are empowered to create reports more efficiently and produce useful insights more efficiently than in a manual reporting environment.

Monitoring and follow-up. Inefficient issue management can tally up hundreds of ill-spent hours for internal auditors. Audit management software enables auditors to streamline the issue management process, from identifying issues to follow-up and reporting. One feature to look for is remediation workflows with automated notifications, which can help internal auditors save time in closing out issues.

The activities described above are scenarios that are supported by quality audit automation software. Later in this chapter, I will discuss what to look for in such software solutions and whether it is the right route for your internal audit team.

Technology Is Essential to Agility

As I noted in chapter 5, the vast majority of internal auditors believe Agile auditing has the potential to add more value to their work compared with traditional approaches — although a substantial percentage believe a lack of knowledge or resources is their most significant obstacle to adopting agile.[4]

Suffice it to say, technology forms the critical backbone of effective Agile internal auditing. Employing technology to automate repetitive manual tasks frees auditors to perform more activities that create value for the business. Technology is also integral to effective collaboration and client involvement. Having a single source of truth for all risk and controls data promotes simplicity and eliminates inefficiencies inherent to a manual audit environment. Specifically, cloud-based platforms with automated notifications power timely insights and responses, more effective and frequent communication between internal audit and its clients, and greater visibility into project status for all stakeholders.

Data Analytics Help Auditors Know Their Business

Data analytics in the context of internal audit typically refers to technology that enables the testing of large data sets, allowing auditors to test full populations, identify anomalies, expand their risk coverage, and provide greater assurance. However, as internal audit faces increased pressure to develop more powerful and data-driven insights, analytics can now refer to a range of data analysis, automation, and business intelligence capabilities. I believe the future of data analytics lies in internal audit successfully harnessing those various capabilities to help organizations continuously monitor organizational risk and drive an integrated risk-first, data-centric approach to auditing. This empowers audit functions to provide real-time assurance, address key risks, and provide valuable insights to the business.

Success in today's data-first environment is nearly impossible without having a centralized system of record. Any effort to employ data analytics to drive assurance and quality insights is useless without reliable data. As PwC noted in a recent *State of the Internal Audit Profession* report: "Organizations cannot make the best use of emerging technologies without trustworthy data — meaning, data that is clean, accurate, and accessible."[6]

If your organization has not yet digitized its audit program, begin by unifying your audit, risk, and compliance data in a system of record that serves as the single source of truth and can integrate with data sources used by other departments. If your organization is already using a data analytics solution, look for an audit management solution that can integrate with it. Finally, it is important to recognize that maturing your business's data analytics capabilities is an ongoing process that often takes years. Approach the process incrementally and seek solutions that can integrate with other technologies your business employs so that they can grow with you.

Employing Emerging Technologies Is Crucial to Leading Change

In addition to audit automation platforms, innovative internal audit functions are increasingly leveraging emerging technologies. One example is automated controls testing, especially for control areas that are standardized, such as where tickets and fields are consistently used.

Robotics process automation (RPA) provides an elegant use of technology for such tasks. RPA technology entails the use of bots and software applications that can be programmed to perform basic human tasks that are typically rote or manual in nature. The main benefit of utilizing RPA in internal audit processes is that a bot can take care of repetitive manual tasks, freeing up time for auditors to perform more value-add activities. Areas where RPA can make the biggest impact in creating efficiencies for internal audit include:

- Data gathering and cleansing for analytics.
- Data gathering and classification for risk assessments (also inherent in audit automation software).
- Processing data populations during initial evidence gathering for controls.
- Internal audit project management areas (also inherent in audit automation software).

Artificial Intelligence: The Technology Elephant in the Room

As anyone in business should be aware of by now, AI simulates human decision-making and thinking by using sophisticated algorithms that learn based on transactions they are fed. In November 2022, the introduction of ChatGPT as a publicly available generative AI application provided an historic jumpstart for applying AI to myriad business activities. Internal audit is no exception.

In October 2023, I published a blog post with AuditBoard Sr. Director of Risk Solutions Anand Bhakta that made a compelling case for leveraging AI in internal audit. Its key messages also capture how internal auditors can act as agents of change, embracing a lead role in helping their organizations understand and leverage emerging risks and technologies. Below are parts of that blog post relevant to any discussion about embracing this evolving technology:

> "It's been under a year since OpenAI launched ChatGPT in November 2022. In that brief time, the rapid adoption of generative artificial intelligence (AI) across industries, regions, and demographics has been remarkable. An April 2023 McKinsey Global Survey — only six months in — found 79% of respondents reporting exposure to generative AI, 22% regularly using it in their work, and 33% whose organizations were using it in at least one function.

Generative AI has hit critical mass at a pace unmatched by any technology in history. Indeed, its entire life cycle has proceeded at warp speed, with regulatory activity (e.g., EU's AI Act; calls for US oversight) and academic studies on the impacts are well underway. But in most organizations, AI risk management and governance are not keeping pace.

With risks emerging and changing faster than ever, internal audit is uniquely positioned to offer insight and foresight. So why are so few internal auditors taking bold, decisive action to help their organizations understand, use, govern, and gain assurance on generative AI? Amid a world racing to embrace AI, are internal auditors at risk of becoming laggards? What's behind the lack of action, and how can we fix it?

AI Use and Governance: Current State

Many organizations are diving headfirst on AI, but few seem prepared to govern its use or manage its risks. McKinsey's study found that 55% of all organizations have adopted some form of AI, and leading organizations are going all-in on generative AI. But only 21% have policies governing employee use of generative AI, and most aren't working to mitigate top generative-AI-related risks. For example, only 38% of organizations are mitigating related cybersecurity risk, 32% inaccuracy, 25% IP infringement, 20% personal/individual privacy, 16% organizational reputation, and 13% workforce/labor displacement.

AuditBoard's pending 2024 Focus on the Future survey, conducted August/September 2023 (coming out in November), offers a somber echo of McKinsey's April findings. Only one in four internal audit leaders said their organizations have defined the risks of, or created guidelines for, its use of AI, and only two in five had a clear understanding of how AI is being used in their organizations. At most, 10% of internal auditors are using generative AI in any way in their own work, and 50–75% have not made any efforts to explore or implement generative AI in internal audit.

A Useful Analogy: Cloud Computing

Many internal auditors are interested and engaged with generative AI. So what explains the lagging use and focus? In part, lack of expertise and resources: A 2022 AuditBoard-Chartered IIA report found that 49% of internal audit leaders cited "lack of skills and competencies" as the top barrier to internal audit adoption of data analytics and AI, followed by 24% citing 'cost/lack of resources.' But we also suspect a general discomfort and pressing need for assurance.

Such was the case in cloud computing's early days. Initially, many regulators — especially in financial services — viewed it as unproven and risky, and banks were slow to adopt. Cloud computing needed to provide a level of assurance around its security, stability, and integrity. Internal audit needed to learn about and validate cloud capabilities and safeguards. Today, cloud is an acknowledged competitive advantage embraced by both banks and regulators.

A similar pattern may be emerging with AI. Businesses rightly worry about accuracy, reliability, security, and more. But discomfort and inexperience shouldn't keep internal audit from taking action. Just as AI technologies must step up to provide a level of assurance, internal audit must also step up. We must educate ourselves, our leaders, and our boards on AI's threats and opportunities, and be bold in helping to determine how best to set up AI processes, controls, and governance.

Guidance is available, and more will emerge. The IIA's 2017 pioneering and still-relevant Artificial Intelligence — Considerations for the Profession of Internal Auditing was supplemented in 2023 by The Artificial Intelligence Revolution (Part 1: Understanding, Adopting, and Adapting to AI; Part 2: Revisiting The IIA's Artificial Intelligence Framework). ISACA's guidance includes 2020's Auditing Guidelines for Artificial Intelligence and 2018's Auditing Artificial Intelligence. Returning to our analogy, the latter suggests early cloud audits as a useful frame of reference for AI auditing (e.g., focusing on in-place controls and business/IT governance aspects).

Bridging the Gap Between AI and Humans
AI is not trying to replace you. Indeed, most internal auditors are confident the role will always require a human touch: in the AuditBoard-Chartered IIA report, less than 3% of internal audit leaders were "very concerned" advanced AI could replace them. ChatGPT itself says we'll always be needed.

AI is simply offering a toolkit and better starting point, freeing you up to spend more time on proactive strategy, risk management, and high-impact decision-making. We see AI as a capacity multiplier and magnifier for human intelligence. As AI automates routine tasks and surfaces insights from ever larger pools of data, human judgment and expertise is critical for understanding nuance, formulating opinions, and developing actionable recommendations."[7]

Integrated Risk Management: The Key to Building Strong Relationships

While improving internal audit processes using AI, automation software and future emerging technologies is a noble and appealing goal, it is important to consider an integrated approach. Rather than simply thinking of how to improve audit life- cycle processes, forward-thinking internal auditors should consider how risk is managed across the entire organization.

The research and advisory firm Gartner defines integrated risk management (IRM) as "a set of practices and processes supported by a risk-aware culture and enabling technologies that improve decision-making and performance through an integrated view of how well an organization manages its unique set of risks." For the organization to understand the full scope of its risks, there should be a comprehensive view of risks across all business units and risk and compliance functions, as well as key business partners, suppliers, and outsourced entities.[8] An IRM approach is beneficial in reducing siloed risk domains and supports dynamic business decision-making via risk-data correlations and shared risk processes.

Developing this understanding fundamentally requires the collaboration of internal audit, risk, and security leaders, which is why a fully integrated approach to risk management is highly compatible with a combined assurance effort. Audit, risk, and compliance leaders who successfully deploy a cohesive IRM approach, supported by enabling technologies that can talk to one another via data integrations, can greatly expand risk coverage and empower their organizations to act on risks in real time.

Creating Time Is Creating Value

So why aren't more organizations joining companies such as UBSI in adopting promising new technologies? Part of the problem lies in the short-sighted view that both technology investment and internal audit generally are considered cost centers rather than value creators. Indeed, I have often lamented that internal audit is wrongly among the first to see cutbacks during economic downturns.

It is important that organizations recognize that technology investment in internal audit can be a capacity multiplier when done strategically, and internal auditors must be prepared to make the case on the return on technology investments. This is where having a change-agent mindset helps. We know the technology exists to make internal audit more effective and efficient, so we must be **bold enough** to advocate for the change and investment that create value.

Ultimately, internal audit leaders can make a compelling case by clearly articulating where an automation solution can save administrative hours in their audit workflows and identify where those saved hours would be redirected. Equating these resource hours to savings or increased productivity helps to build an even stronger case. After all, creating time is creating value.

How to Begin Building a Change-Enabling Foundation

One of the biggest takeaways from this chapter should be that having the right technology in place is foundational to enabling change that creates value. Internal auditors who are still performing their engagements manually should prioritize digitizing their audit program by unifying their audit, risk, and compliance data. A best practice is to seek a technology solution that:

- Enables remote collaboration with team members, stakeholders, and consultants and external auditors.
- Serves as the single source of truth for all audit, risk, and controls data.
- Has end-to-end automated workflows from planning to testing to reporting and issue management.
- Enables and empowers integrated risk management and combined assurance.

While various platforms offer differing features, the following are basic qualities that any leading technology solution should have:

Deep domain expertise. Whether it is Slack for instant messaging or Zoom for unified video communication, enterprises have found greater value from using software solutions that are purpose-built for specific departments, use cases, or industries, versus one-size-fits-all solutions. The marketplace now provides a wide variety of ideal options that address the nuanced needs of individual teams and can integrate with other solutions.

Bottom-up product development. User experience is key. Best-in-class solutions today employ a "bottom-up" product development approach focused on use cases specific to the department and are consequently optimized for the end users. This approach positions all members of an organization or team to successfully use the product. The software industry has seen that products with the best user experience typically have the best adoption and engagement rates.

Intuitive user experience. Optimizing technology must also consider ease of use to extract valuable data and insights in real time. Best-in-class technology solutions are designed to automate manual processes, consolidate data into a core system of record, and be flexible enough to manipulate and configure data into key insights, reports, and dashboards that support high-impact business decisions. Although this is true across all enterprise software solutions, it is especially relevant for audit, risk, and compliance software, whose users are facing increasing pressure to deliver risk-first, data-driven insights to executive management for agile decision-making. This requires solutions that are intuitive for the user.

Optimized for collaboration. As enterprises become increasingly connected, the ability for various users across the business to collaborate in a platform has increased in importance. Cloud-based solutions that are built to integrate with other cloud technologies, including Microsoft 365, Slack, and Google Suite, are highly valuable because they enable users to work within the native platforms they prefer while maximizing the potential of department-specific software. Additionally, solutions that embrace connectivity and collaboration resonate much better with customers.

The COVID-19 pandemic that emerged in 2020 fundamentally altered how people work on a day-to-day basis, and it clearly demonstrated just how integral technology is to the survival of modern business. While internal auditors may have been slowly moving toward more integrated platforms prior to the crisis, the rapid shift to a fully remote workforce highlights the need for technology that enables organizationwide collaboration and automates administrative activities. As our profession inexorably moves from manual to automated audit engagements, those who understand and embrace technology as an enabler of value creation will lead our profession as true agents of change.

Chapter 7

Agents of Change Aren't Secret Agents

The greatest discovery of all time is that a person can change his future by merely changing his attitude.

— Oprah Winfrey —

Anyone who spends time with the best internal auditors will quickly discern that there is a quiet passion that drives them. It is built on a genuine desire to help their organizations, respect from those with whom they interact, and unwavering pride in the service they provide. These characteristics — passion, desire, earned respect, and pride — are in the DNA of internal audit change agents.

Yet, even among top performers in our field, many struggle to communicate what they do and how their work adds value for their organizations. This challenge is so commonplace in the profession that we've learned to joke about it. Take the one about the man who instructs his child to tell his classmates that he works at McDonald's, because it's easier than explaining he is an internal auditor.

This self-deprecating attitude is pervasive and can be counterproductive to achieving the status of change agents in the eyes of our stakeholders. The profession is damaged by just this kind of misguided humility and reticence, which I saw time and again among my peers as I traveled the world as president and CEO of The IIA between 2009 and 2021.

In contrast, agents of change successfully graduate from simply telling their own story to reshaping how the profession is seen. They are excellent storytellers who can inspire confidence and build trust. Indeed, while at Spotify's Kenneth Chen identified the ability to be influential and effectively communicate the top skill he looked for when hiring managers for his audit function.

Recasting the Internal Audit Story

To formulate internal audit's story, we can begin with a gap analysis: Identify where we are and where we want to be in the eyes of our stakeholders and the general public. However, accurately identifying how internal audit is currently perceived can be tricky. There are many variables that influence the view, including differences in industry, organization size, complexity, and maturity; the level of regulation, compliance, and competition; the portfolio of risks most relevant to each organization; vulnerability to disruptive innovation; and the economic model under which organizations operate.

The easier part of the gap analysis is to identify where we want to be. So, let us begin there. Imagine a scenario in which internal audit's value to organizations is clearly and commonly understood. This is not as hard as one might think, mostly because a lot of the thinking has already been done for us. As I noted earlier in the book, The IIA's 2030 vision statement helped crystalize where we want to be as a profession: *Internal audit professionals are universally recognized as indispensable to effective governance, risk management, and control.*

That serves as a sound starting point. But I would argue that we need to take the vision one step further. Not only should the profession be recognized as indispensable to effective governance, risk management, and control, it also should be recognized as an indispensable element of value creation within the organization. So, we have set a lofty goal; now let's see how close we are to achieving it.

Is Indispensable Within Reach?

There is little debate that reliable assurance over the effectiveness of governance, risk management, and control adds value to an organization, and that a sufficiently resourced, independent internal audit function can deliver it. To be sure, as risk challenges become more complex and the speed of risk accelerates, stakeholders are increasingly attuned to the value of assurance. Therefore, identifying where stakeholders turn for assurance provides part of the answer to whether internal audit is considered indispensable.

The IIA's 2021 *OnRisk* report provided a unique examination of risk as viewed by internal audit *and* its stakeholders. Through qualitative and quantitative surveys, it examined the perspectives of the board, C-suite, and internal audit on key risks. The survey for *OnRisk 2021* asked where organizations turn to for assurance. The results were decidedly mixed.

While a significant majority of CAEs said they provided or anticipated providing assurance over cybersecurity, third-party risks, business continuity and crisis management, and data governance, their attention to other key risks quickly fell off, as shown in **exhibit 7-1**.

Exhibit 7-1
Assurance Conversation

On average, CAEs provide assurance on 4 or 5 of the risks listed below — most commonly cybersecurity, third party, business continuity/crisis management, and data governance.

Q7. Which of the following risks do you provide or anticipate providing assurance on in 2020 and/or 2021? (Multi-Select)

Risk	Percentage
Cybersecurity	84%
Third party	71%
Business continuity & crisis management	71%
Data governance	66%
Organizational governance	45%
Board information	24%
Talent management	23%
Culture	21%
Sustainability	19%
Disruptive innovation	14%
Economic & political volatility	11%
None of the above	3%

But when we compared the levels of assurance to those risks that the C-suite and boards identified as most relevant, internal audit was off the mark. At that time, C-suite and board respondents ranked talent management and culture as the second- and third-most relevant risks, while fewer than a quarter of CAEs reported providing assurance in these two areas, as illustrated in **exhibit 7-2**.[2]

Exhibit 7-2
Organizational Relevance

Immediately we see that relevance is usually rated higher than capability and knowledge, especially for cybersecurity.

● C-SUITE   ● BOARD   ○ CAEs

Category	
Cybersecurity	
Third party	
Board information	
Sustainability	
Disruptive innovation	
Economic & political volatility	
Organizational governance	
Data governance	
Talent management	
Culture	
Business continuity & crisis management	

0% 10% 20% 30% 40% 50% 60% 70% 80% 90% 100%

More recent data suggest internal audit assurance gaps continue. In 2023, PwC's Global CEO survey identified inflation and macroeconomic volatility as the top two risks.[3] Yet, PwC's Global Internal Audit Study 2023 found "that nearly 50% of IA functions are not addressing these two top threats in their audit plan, and one in 10 have no plans to do so at all."[4]

The real shame of it is the same PwC study, which surveyed 4,680 internal audit leaders and stakeholders globally, found "that many business leaders want more strategic engagement with IA [internal audit] early and proactively with 68% wanting IA to be involved during the risk identification and assessment stage and over 50% seeking IA involvement in management strategy and planning."[5]

The good news is that business leaders would like to turn to internal audit for assurance and strategic engagement in key risk areas. The bad news is that the work of far too many internal audit functions is not aligned with stakeholders' assurance desires.

Ironically, one could argue that internal audit stakeholders increasingly recognize its value and possibly see it as indispensable in the current dynamic risk environment. However, if we continue to fall short on providing assurance services in risk areas stakeholders find most relevant, they will seek such assurance elsewhere. Internal audit's reputation must be one that promotes the value of timely, relevant, and independent assurance. So, it is here where we must focus on telling our story.

Forging an Effective Communication Strategy

Managing reputations and earning trust are significant challenges. The first step to forging an effective communication strategy is to have better understanding of both.

Telling people what we do and convincing them of its value would seem to be a simple and straightforward task. After all, we carry out our jobs daily and know each step in our audit engagements. However, knowing our profession and effectively communicating how it helps the organization achieve its goals are vastly different things. What's more, as Spotify's Kenneth Chen noted, the challenge is more than just telling people about internal audit, it's about "selling" them on the value of internal audit.

There are any number of ways to look at reputation, but for our purposes here, a simple dictionary definition will suffice: Reputation is a widespread belief that someone or something has a particular habit or characteristic. Influencing any widespread belief is a complex endeavor that requires not just setting a clear and concise message — *internal audit is indispensable to good governance, risk management, and control* — but also persuading the audience of that message's validity, relevance, and accuracy.

The Principles of Persuasion[6] offered by Influence at Work provides some intriguing insights into how to influence what others think, which is ultimately what we want to accomplish with an effective communication strategy. Influence at Work breaks down the art of persuasion into six key principles: reciprocity, authority, consistency, liking, consensus, and scarcity. By applying the six principles to internal audit, we can begin forging our strategy.

Chapter 7: Agents of Change Aren't Secret Agents

1. **Reciprocity.** Be the first to give, and make sure it is personal and unexpected.

   This principle taps into the positive feelings created when someone receives a pleasant surprise. Internal audit practitioners can accomplish this by telling clients not just what's wrong but also what's right.

2. **Authority.** People follow the lead of credible, knowledgeable experts.

   Keeping stakeholders informed of the internal audit team's credentials and certifications builds its reputation as a source of expertise. Even something as simple as mentioning an audit team's years of experience or number of IIA certifications during introductory meetings can help build authority.

3. **Consistency.** Looking for small but voluntary, active, and public commitments can lead to greater commitments.

   This can apply to getting clients to openly agree to adopt easily implemented audit recommendations, such as posting in the breakroom a list of tips on how to avoid and report phishing emails. This will make it easier to accept recommendations in the future for weightier actions, such as implementing formal anti-phishing training.

4. **Liking.** People are more likely to like things that are viewed as similar, complimentary, and cooperative.

   Building relationships with clients outside of formal engagements helps put a familiar face on internal audit. Assigning specific teams or managers to work exclusively with certain departments can help build rapport and likeability without sacrificing independence or objectivity.

5. **Consensus.** People look to the actions of others to determine their own.

   Liking can help build consensus. As more audit clients learn to appreciate and collaborate with internal audit, others will follow suit.

6. Scarcity. People want more of those things they can have less of. Communicate the unique benefit and what they stand to lose.

   This principle requires an existing awareness of internal audit's value. In some organizations, less internal audit would be viewed as a positive! However, once internal audit builds authority and consensus, and demonstrates its value, communicating the consequences should internal audit be cut will be easier.

Formally Updating Our Story

A leading practice that I have promoted to CAEs for many years is to periodically produce a report on internal audit's performance and accomplishments. Such periodic disclosures were mandated when I was a U.S. government inspector general. But generating such reports is also widely practiced in the private sector. Whether produced annually or more frequently, these reports reaffirm to our stakeholders the value we are delivering for the organization.

One of the world's most respected companies, Coca-Cola, uses an annual Stewardship Report prepared by the corporate audit department to update stakeholders. Barry Ballow, CAE at Coca-Cola, said he incorporates four pillars into his annual report: quality, people, capability, and productivity/innovation. Here's how he does it.

Quality. This part of the report identifies the improvements the department made during the past year, particularly as they applied to IIA *Standards* quality assurance self-assessments. It also includes stakeholder feedback. In short, it communicates how and why internal audit is doing a good job.

People. This updates stakeholders on certifications earned, new hires, and pro- motions. It includes assessment of staff by those outside of internal audit as well, such as an engagement survey within the company.

Capability. Here, the audit department tracks advancements in team capabilities and provides an update on its digital journey. For example, it includes details on the use of tools, such as process mining, new and different digital approaches, and improved access and use of data.

Productivity/innovation. Of particular focus is the section in Coca-Cola's Stewardship Report that addresses the internal audit function's effectiveness. It covers budget and headcount, and maps those measures against maintaining high quality and investing in digital capability. It addresses improvements in processes, such as Agile auditing; automation, such as the use of dashboards populated directly from data software; and the strategy of leveraging all department resources globally.

"It's a bit of a marketing tool, but it is important to market the value add," Ballow said. "People understand our role in governance, that we are a required function in a large, publicly traded company. What they don't see is how we are innovative, how we are driving improvements, and how we are not immune to different stresses that they are feeling."

By recognizing the tools and techniques available to influence reputation, then applying them to daily actions, processes, and reports, such as Coca-Cola's Stewardship Report, we can begin to forge a strategy on reputation.

As a federal inspector general, I had a statutory obligation to update my agency, Congress, and the public on the work of our organization semiannually. Those reports could have simply been a sparse and unassuming recounting of the number of audits and investigations we undertook during the preceding six months. But like many of my fellow IGs, I recognized the opportunity that the reports presented to "tell our story" as an office of inspector general (OIG). So, our reports were well-produced, attractive chronologies of our progress in fostering efficiency, economy, and effectiveness within the agency. I also took the time to personally add to our story. I signed my last semiannual report as inspector general of the Tennessee Valley Authority (TVA), a federally owned corporation that provides power and other services to millions in the southeastern United States, in October 2001. In my cover letter, I wrote:

> "Consistent with our newly adopted strategic plan, we made significant progress during the period in aligning the organization to better support the needs of our stakeholders. In this regard, we reorganized our audit operations to provide better emphasis on the core business processes of TVA, including energy operations. In addition, we created a separate team to provide advisory services to TVA officials and members of Congress with questions about TVA operations. We also realigned our investigative resources to facilitate our role in ensuring integrity in TVA operations.
>
> "We have featured the United States flag on the cover of this report as a reflection of our sympathy and solidarity with those directly affected by the tragic events beginning with the September 11, 2001, terrorist attacks on America. We stand ready to assist fellow law enforcement agencies in any way possible during this time of national crisis."[7]

The report went on to highlight the work of the OIG during the period, and included insight into our strategic planning process, highlights of audits and investigations undertaken, and honors and accolades bestowed on the TVA OIG by other federal organizations. Our objective in producing the report was to create awareness about our effectiveness in executing our statutory oversight mission, and to inspire confidence in our key stakeholders.[8] We were — simply — telling our story.

Communication and Marketing

A facet that complicates internal audit's struggles with improving its reputation is that many in the profession see any attempt to promote or communicate our value as unseemly. There has always been an aversion among internal auditors to come off as used-car salesmen. Yet, we see examples of two top companies, Spotify and Coca-Cola, where effective marketing of internal audit has led to greater success. In fact, I do not consider such initiatives to be "marketing" at all. Instead, I view it as awareness creation — a vital responsibility if we are to ensure our stakeholders understand our mission and potential in serving our organizations.

Every internal audit function can and should embrace techniques and practices to create awareness about its value and reputation, including:

- Holding one-on-one conversations with stakeholders — both formally and informally — where internal audit can solicit feedback.
- Developing professional presentations about the internal audit department through brochures, PowerPoint presentations, or intranet sites.
- Periodic reports on internal audit accomplishments, strategies, clarifications, and announcements, such as Coca-Cola's Stewardship Report.

But an even more fundamental practice is to educate internal audit practitioners to speak clearly and proudly about what we do. We should know instinctively what distinguishes us as a profession and be ready to declare it proudly. It is in that spirit that I offer a list of key messages to use if someone asked on an elevator, "What is it you do?"

- *"I am an internal auditor!"* This first line should be pretty self-explanatory. We should be proud and confident about being internal auditors. Few professions offer the opportunities to contribute to the success of our organizations like internal auditing does.

- *"I serve my organization to protect and enhance its value."* We're not just here to guard the doors and make sure people don't walk off with the assets. We're not just here to make sure others are not breaking the rules. We're here to make sure the organization achieves its objectives and creates value for shareholders/stakeholders.

- *"I model integrity, objectivity, confidentiality, and competency every day."* These are taken from the four elements of The IIA's Code of Ethics. This is what we stand for as a profession, and it is something every practitioner should exhibit with every engagement and interaction.

- *"I improve risk management, internal controls, and governance in my organization."* This is at the heart of the definition of internal auditing articulated in the International Professional Practices Framework (IPPF). The definition speaks to adding value and improving an organization's operations. Simply, we make our organizations better.

- *"I follow The IIA's Standards when providing assurance and advice."* All professions have to have standards. They are what set individuals apart as professionals. That is why we must follow the *Standards*, to ensure the quality is there. I also urge internal auditors who have earned IIA certifications to proudly speak out. One should not be shy about proclaiming, "I am certified by The IIA to demonstrate the proficiency I have for carrying out my responsibilities as a professional internal auditor." As noted earlier in the chapter, authority is one of the principles of persuasion.

- *"I am respected and admired because I am a guardian of trust!"* This is a wonderful claim for any professional to make. Every internal auditor may not be respected and admired as a guardian of trust, but that should be their aspiration.

Those six simple messages shouldn't be viewed as a creed to be recited every time we're asked what we do. Instead, they should be used to add a little color to our description of internal auditing. They reveal an inspired and impassioned profession that is committed to making organizations better. We should be proud of what we do, and we should communicate that every day.

This brings us to one of the most difficult challenges in improving internal audit's reputation. Often, we can be our own worst enemy.

The Humble Internal Auditor

Part of the indoctrination into all cultures is the fundamental concept of acceptable behavior or social norms. One that is present in nearly all cultures is the concept of collaboration. From a young age, we are taught that we can accomplish more through cooperation and partnership. In short, we are told to "play well with others." Implicit in that social norm is the concept of humility. Simply, humility is having or showing a modest or low estimate of one's own importance and that, in order to "play well with others," we must check our egos at the door.

But humility can be deceivingly complex. Nihar Chhaya, a corporate executive coach who has advised senior leaders at many global companies, addressed humility in leadership in a recent *Forbes* magazine article, offering a concise and insightful definition. Humility is not about avoiding recognition of our strengths.

In other words, being humble is not about putting yourself down; it's about recognizing that, despite your strengths and weaknesses, accomplishments, and mistakes, you don't deserve any different treatment than anyone else.[9]

Chhaya bases his definition in part on the views of German entrepreneur Karl Albrecht, who sees humility as achieving emotional neutrality and overcoming a natural "competitive reflex." A closer examination of Albrecht's discussion on humility provides additional insight into what humility "is not." Consonant with the premise of what humility is not, as I think of it:

- It's not letting others "push you around."
- It's not being a doormat, a sucker, or letting people "walk all over you."
- It's not constantly sacrificing your interests to those of others (and then feeling like a victim or a martyr).
- It's not avoiding conflict or confrontation — not of your making, anyway — for the sake of "being nice."
- It's not about hiding your feelings or suppressing your views to avoid alienating others.[10]

Ironically, Albrecht's treatment of the topic actually makes the case that humility is underrated and misunderstood. He blames that partly on a "popular-media culture (that) is saturated with themes of conflict, combat, and conquest. Popular films feature cops chasing crooks; the military fighting terrorists; the lone avenger pursuing the evildoers. We say we love peace makers, but our heroes are warriors. As a society, we like our celebrities to be cheeky, self-important, and even a bit narcissistic."[11]

He goes on to say that our society categorizes those who are genuinely humble as a bit strange. From an internal audit perspective, outsiders may indeed see us as a bit strange, or at least existing apart from the mainstream workforce. We are largely to blame for this misperception. We wrap ourselves in the flags of independence and objectivity, shield ourselves from the rest of the organization, and think of this as a virtue. Instead, it can be a straitjacket that limits our ability to elevate the profession in the eyes of our stakeholders.

As Coca-Cola's Ballow noted, "Humility and all of that is great, but we are in a business. It's important that we communicate our value to the business."

You can't raise awareness if you are unwilling to speak up about your accomplishments. You can't rise above the din of a host of others clamoring to be heard if you don't "toot your own horn." You can't expect busy stakeholders to seek out or single out your service and counsel if you don't even show up on their radar. In short, you can't be a change agent if you're a secret agent.

Promoting and Provoking Change

I have made the case that telling our story must include a sound strategy that raises awareness and appreciation for the value of independent assurance and builds trust among our stakeholders about our skills as individual practitioners. An important subtext to this strategy is not just understanding but embracing the concept that effectively telling our story is not boastful, arrogant, or inappropriate. Indeed, being an effective promoter of internal audit should be a part of every practitioner's DNA.

By raising awareness and building trust, we set the foundation for stakeholders to recognize the unique and informed perspective of internal audit. Implicit in this willingness to promote the profession must be a commitment to deliver outstanding service.

In *Trusted Advisors*, I explored the key attributes of practitioners who have achieved the title status. At the end of the book, I shared a list of definitions of trusted advisors offered by top internal audit leaders around the world. Those definitions capture key elements of high-performing practitioners.

When it comes to outstanding internal auditors, the difference is not a matter of what but how. It is not that they do entirely different things; it's that they perform these practices in an outstanding way.

And along the way, they earn trust. They listen to others, they keep their self-interest under control, they display empathy, they share credit, they build relationships, they seek more complete solutions, and they focus on supporting the business. They have their eyes on the future and their feet in the present. Most of all, they cherish and protect the trust they earn, because they are well aware how quickly it can be lost.[12]

Agents of change take this concept one step further. They are the top performers, the *trusted advisors*, who recognize they can promote and foster change within their organizations. Agents of change understand that change begets change, and they are comfortable articulating how they can foster change. They build a culture of change by continually pushing to innovate. And they are never satisfied with the status quo.

Part Three

The Right Stuff

Chapter 8

Business Acumen

Either you're an agent of change or destined to become a victim of change. You simply can't survive over the long term if you insist on standing still.

— Norm Brodsky —

The overarching theme of this book revolves around change. In part one, I focused on how the internal audit profession came to be, how it has evolved over its storied history, and why radical transformation is imperative for the profession in today's volatile risk environment. Part two offered a frank assessment on the dire need to shift our attitudes and approaches in the key areas of process, agility, technology, and communications. In this final part, I address the individual practitioner and what is required to increase the ranks of agents of change within our profession.

In *Trusted Advisors,* I wrote extensively about the attributes it takes for internal auditors to become genuine "trusted advisors" within their organizations. I believe becoming a trusted advisor is critical to ultimately becoming an agent of change. As internal audit practitioners advance through their careers, they must see their journey as an evolution of skills, a consistent series of successes in executing on those skills, and building a reputation for excellence that elevates them in the eyes of key stakeholders.

That requires practitioners to not just possess deep knowledge and know how to communicate it, but also have the wherewithal to facilitate change on the basis of that knowledge. I've referred to this as having "The Right Stuff," borrowing the phrase from the 1979 Tom Wolfe book of the same name. The book was an homage to test pilots engaged in U.S. postwar research with experimental aircraft. It was from the ranks of those pilots that the first Project Mercury astronauts were selected for the NASA space program. While few internal auditors will have the opportunity to shriek beyond the speed of sound or venture into outer space, there are parallels between those daring test pilots and internal auditors who have the courage and willingness to take on the unknown to advance the profession and, more importantly, improve their organizations.

As I noted, understanding the *how* in addition to the *what* is vital, which I addressed in the introduction to *Trusted Advisors*:

> *I believe that becoming a trusted advisor involves not just what you know (risk, control, and governance expertise) but also how you get things done (relationship acumen). Both are valuable attributes for internal auditors to possess, but it is only through their combination that one can truly become a trusted advisor.*
>
> *I've witnessed two internal auditors perform similar actions with very different outcomes. I suspect the reason is that the less effective internal auditor is strong in one trait and deficient in the other. Perhaps he has a strong technical background in internal auditing but can't communicate in a way that resonates with others. In fact, he may just be painful to work with. Or maybe he is a delightful lunch companion — humorous, charming, talkative — but with very little of substance to say. Excellence requires a balance of technical and soft skills.*
>
> *Internal auditors who rise above challenges and obstacles have achieved that balance by building a broad portfolio of complementary traits and attributes. These select few are not infallible — no one is perfect — but most do find success, and when they don't, they learn from their mistakes, avoid repeating them, and move on.*

Trusted Advisors goes on to examine nine of the most desirable attributes of outstanding auditors based on a survey of members of The IIA's Audit Leaders Network (formerly Audit Executive Center). Those traits are ethical resilience, results-focused, intellectual curiosity, open mindedness, dynamic communication, insightful relationships, inspirational leadership, critical thinking, and technical expertise. A similar global survey of internal audit leaders for *Agents of Change* found considerable overlap in key attributes. Indeed, the top attribute identified in the survey for this book — business acumen — is a powerful combination of many of the attributes I explored in *Trusted Advisors* (see **exhibit 8-1**).

Exhibit 8-1
Key Attributes of Change Agents

Attribute	Percentage
Other	
Tech savvy	9%
Inspirational	9%
Detail-oriented	10%
Intellectual curiosity	19%
Navigates internal politics	29%
Industry knowledge	30%
Courage	33%
Innovative	38%
Dynamic communicator	44%
Strategic	48%
Enterprise perspective	53%
Relationship builder	57%
Understands organizational objectives	59%
Business acumen	60%

Note: Q10: What are the most important attributes an internal auditor must demonstrate to be a successful Agent of Change? n = 606

Candidly, possessing business acumen is fundamental for anyone aspiring to reach the highest levels of any profession, including internal auditing. Over my long career, I have seen how the elements of business acumen shape the success of internal auditors and how weaknesses in this area have held back others. I addressed business acumen briefly in *Trusted Advisors*, and that discussion provides a good foundation for understanding this attribute. This excerpt focuses on the value of strong business acumen and why it should be understood both generally (at the macro level) and at the enterprise level. Both are essential to being a true agent of change.

> *Generally speaking, individuals who possess business acumen are perceived to consistently exercise sound judgment and make decisions that result in favorable outcomes. They can assimilate information from an array of sources and use that new knowledge to propose sound strategic alternatives to address issues and problems. They also are always looking ahead trying to foresee opportunities and threats, the better to develop strategies to remain one step ahead of the competition. Possibly most important, they have the ability to see across the many areas of expertise within a company, such as finance, research and development, marketing, and IT; understand how decisions affect each of these areas; and work toward coordinating efforts to ensure shared success. This trait is called "breadth of understanding,"[1] and it was called out specifically in the AEC survey responses as a skill that can be achieved only by conscious effort and one that must be "continuously worked on."*

A more succinct definition of business acumen is "keenness and quickness in understanding and dealing with a business situation in a manner that is likely to lead to a good outcome."[2] That definition packs a great deal of subtle meaning and demands into a mere 23 words. It requires *keenness, quickness,* and *understanding*. Therefore, for someone to display business acumen, they must be willing and eager to quickly learn enough about business to not only comprehend and grasp the subject, but to do so in a way that is likely to lead to a good outcome. That final requirement identifies a level of knowledge, insight, and sophistication that improves the chances of success.

General Business Acumen

Much has been written on business acumen. There are extensive descriptions as to what it constitutes. But in the end, I believe there are five elements critical to the fundamental process of how all organizations operate. Generally, they address finances, marketplace, operations, technology, and strategy. I believe that a keen understanding about each of these areas constitutes business acumen.

1. **Financial acumen.** This involves the metrics of business performance used to gauge success. It includes understanding and interpreting income statements, balance sheets, cash flow reports, forecasting

and modeling, and other tools and techniques to track the financial health of the organization.

2. **Marketplace acumen.** This encompasses knowledge and understanding of competition, market drivers, consumer needs, marketing, disruptive innovation, and other influences on business success. It is critical to defining, creating, projecting, and protecting brand and reputation.

3. **Operational acumen.** This requires understanding factors that influence day-to-day operations and production, including the supply chain, third-party relationships, quality assurance, process improvement, and other systems that make the business run.

4. **Technology acumen.** This is the newest entrant to the components of business acumen, but it will likely grow quickly in importance. As we advance inexorably into the digital age, understanding how to leverage technology will be fundamental to the success of every organization. What's more, possessing technology skillsets — for example, understanding basic software program coding — to support the other components of business acumen will soon be as familiar and expected as Excel or PowerPoint skills were 10 years ago.

5. **Strategic acumen.** Probably the most important aspect of business acumen is recognizing and understanding the systems that define and influence an organization's goals and direction. In concert, they define business strategy, which drives operations, finances, and marketing. These systems include risk management; decision making; data gathering, analysis, and use; short- and long-term planning; talent management; organizational culture; and more.

I will delve deeper into strategic acumen in the next chapter.[3, 4]

In chapter 3, we examined the list of skills identified in the change agent survey. This examination included grouping those skills into three categories — professional, personal, and relational. Many of the characteristics identified in the professional category apply to general business acumen. Indeed, four of the top five attributes of change agents speak directly to it — business acumen, understanding organizational objectives, enterprisewide perspectives, and strategic (see **exhibit 8-2**).

Exhibit 8-2
Skills Categories

Professional	Personal	Relational
Business acumen (1)	Innovative (7)	Relationship builder (3)
Understands organizational objectives (2)	Courage (8)	Navigates internal politics (10)
Enterprisewide perspective (4)	Intellectual curiosity (11)	Dynamic communicator (6)
Strategic (5)	Detail-oriented (12)	
Industry knowledge (9)	Inspirational (13)	
Tech savvy (14)		

That suggests survey respondents put a premium on the building blocks of general business acumen as core competencies of internal auditors who make the best change agents. In other words, those internal auditors who wish to drive organizational change as a result of their work must be willing to identify and commit to a set of core competencies — and business acumen is chief among them. It goes without saying that people are not born with business acumen. It is a learned skill developed and honed over time, requiring lifelong learning and perseverance. For those who wish to develop or enhance their business acumen, there are several key steps that I would recommend.

Find a mentor. The idea of the student learning at the feet of the master is as old as time itself. In the modern context, having a career guide is critical to learning the finer points of a complex and unforgiving business world. The benefits of having a sounding board and a place where it's safe to be vulnerable and get career advice are substantial, according to leaders at the Wharton School of Management. "It's a relationship where one can let one's guard down, a place where one can get honest feedback, and a place, ideally, where one can get psychological and social support in handling stressful situations," according to Wharton

Management Professor Katherine Klein.[5] Studies consistently show that good mentoring programs benefit both mentors and mentees. Mentoring programs increase employee engagement, and those in such programs are more likely to be promoted. Indeed, they have been proven to increase promotions for mentors and mentees five to six times more than non-participating employees.[6]

However, not every organization has a mentoring program, and poorly designed programs can do more harm than good. For example, a study that examined the protégé perspective found general support for the notion that, on average, bad programs are stronger than good programs in predicting protégé outcomes. A second study looked at the mentor perspective and found mixed support for the prediction that, on average, bad is stronger than good.[7]

So, one shouldn't rely solely on formal mentoring programs. The modern employee-employer relationship tends to be temporary. Unlike the business world I joined as a young internal auditor, few expect to retire from a company with a gold watch and pension after 30 years. Building relationships with an experienced leader outside of formal programs is a valuable option.

Get comfortable with financial statements and strategies. As I mentioned earlier in this chapter, part of developing financial acumen is understanding how money works in business. Digging out the details of finances and strategies can be challenging, but there are several ways to glean the information:

- Publicly traded companies are generally required to report periodically on their organizational structure, equity holdings, subsidiaries, employee stock purchases and savings plans, legal proceedings, controls and procedures, material weaknesses, executive compensation, and more.
- Such reports are often accompanied by quarterly earnings calls, in which company executives address details on strategies and forecasts.
- Annual reports are common to publicly traded and privately held companies. These can provide a great deal of detail on organizational finances.
- Financial information on public-sector organizations — those that operate with public funds — also is readily available. Local,

state/provincial, or federal treasuries typically collect and make available a great deal of information on finances and expenditures.

Pay attention to business news. Business media invest substantial resources to learn and disseminate information about individual companies as well as general business and economic trends. Identifying and closely monitoring credible business news outlets for information is a good practice.

Read, read, read. Whether through quarterly earnings reports, books on business, or biographies on successful entrepreneurs, internal auditors who wish to develop and maintain a healthy business acumen must remain informed.

Commit to lifelong learning. Practitioners must dedicate themselves to not just building core competencies, such as business acumen, they also must nurture and strengthen those competencies once achieved.

Know Your Business

As I have shared frequently over the years, one of the most common complaints I hear from management about internal audit is "they don't know the business." In such cases, management sees internal auditors as book smart on internal controls and risk management, but not street smart on what makes the company run. To truly transcend the ceiling below which management thinks we live, we need to have a deep understanding of our own organizations — regardless of the sector.

Having cultivated strong general business acumen is simply not enough. You must also learn how to apply and leverage that competency within your organization if you have any hope of being an agent of change. Effectively applying business acumen within the parameters of your specific role in the organization while staying true to the Purpose of Internal Auditing, the Global Internal Audit Standards, and ethical guidelines of the profession will be challenging, but it can be done.

The *Business Acumen Handbook* by Steven Haines describes nicely the two dimensions of business acumen, pairing the kinds of acumen already discussed (financial, marketplace, operational, technology, and strategic) with what he refers to as "domain expertise." The latter is what I address in the previous paragraph — applying the value of effective internal auditing to the business. Haines conveniently imagines the concept in a way internal auditors will fine familiar and comforting — a simple quadrant graph where the *y* axis is business acumen and the *x* axis is domain expertise[8] (see **exhibit 8-3**).

Exhibit 8-3
Two-dimensional Business Acumen

[Quadrant graph with BUSINESS ACUMEN on y-axis and DOMAIN EXPERTISE on x-axis]

There are at least three additional competencies a change agent must cultivate: build lasting professional relationships, operate strategically, and become a relentless innovator. I will go into each of these areas in depth in the next three chapters, but we should first examine how they are supported by business acumen at the enterprise level.

Relationship Acumen

Over many years, I have written and spoken extensively about relationship acumen. I rate it on par with business acumen as table stakes for becoming a change agent. As you can imagine, relationship acumen has been the topic of many conversations over my career in internal auditing. One of the most insightful was my discussion with Kevin Patton, director of internal audit for The Ohio State University, who is a staunch supporter of relationship building.

It was his emphasis on the importance of relationship acumen in higher education that sparked an epiphany in me about its role in the agent of change journey. What follows is a short excerpt from *Trusted Advisors* of my conversation with Patton.

"In corporations, the decision-making process is very top-down. The CEO makes a decision, and it is disseminated down through the ranks. In higher education, we have a shared governance model. Faculty, administrators, even students have a say in how the university operates. So working together through relationships is paramount."

Corporate executives who are brought into a university setting, Patton explains, often have trouble making the transition to this shared governance approach. *"Shared governance depends on relationships — and, yes, building those relationships can slow down the process, but it is critical to getting needed buy-in."*[9]

The final point Patton made offers a critical lesson for those who strive to become agents of change. Whether it is persuading others to share governance, share power, or simply earning their trust, learning to build and maintain relationships is critical.

Having solid business acumen supports the change agent's ability to communicate with stakeholders at their level. Understanding the fundamentals of the organization's finances, operations, marketplace, technology, and strategy combined with an enterprisewide perspective on risk, governance, and control place the change agent in a unique position to help the organization achieve its goals. However, if we cannot build relationships with key stakeholders, those skills and competencies are wasted.

Operating Strategically

Earlier in this chapter, I described strategic acumen as recognizing and understanding the systems that define and influence an organization's goals and direction. Those systems are intertwined and influence virtually all aspects of internal audit's work. Change agents not only understand risk management, but they also apply their knowledge of decision-making, short- and long-term planning, talent management, culture, and more to identifying areas where the organization can improve and excel.

Additionally, change agents recognize how those intertwined systems and relationships influence the actions of others within the organization. A critical part of operating strategically is recognizing how and when to take action, respond to challenges, and push for change. I explore the characteristics of the strategic internal auditor in more depth in chapter 9.

Relentless Innovation

To innovate is to make changes in something established, especially by introducing new methods, ideas, or products. This virtually defines the change agent mindset. While internal auditors are not expected to identify new product lines or introduce new technology to the organization, the change agent can leverage his or her business acumen and holistic view of the organization to see and promote such opportunities. Key to innovation is having the flexibility to think entrepreneurially and creatively as well as being willing to consider outside perspectives.

Put simply, internal auditors help the trains run on time. Change agents identify the need for and add new routes.

The Change Agent Value Proposition

Evolution and change must be consistent themes in the lives of change agents. It is logical to assume that the change agent value proposition is an evolution of the more traditional internal audit value proposition.

Some time ago, The IIA published a tool to help practitioners communicate the value of their work to primary stakeholders, including audit committees, boards of directors, management, and audit clients. Represented by three intersecting circles, the value proposition is based on the three core elements of value — assurance, insight, and objectivity — delivered by internal audit to an organization (see **exhibit 8-4).**

Exhibit 8-4
Value Proposition

The 2015 update to the International Professional Practices Framework (IPPF) added a set of Core Principles for the Professional Practice of Internal Auditing. Among them is a requirement for internal audit to be "insightful, proactive, and future-focused." I view this as an important evolution of the insight component of the value proposition. Indeed, this leads me to add *foresight* to the internal audit value proposition.

Now that I've identified internal audit's value proposition as containing three distinct elements — assurance, insight and foresight, and objectivity – let's examine how agents of change can apply business acumen to each of those elements:

> **Assurance = Governance, Risk, and Control.** Internal auditing provides assurance on the organization's governance, risk management, and control processes to help organizations achieve their strategic, operational, financial, and compliance objectives.
>
> **Insight and Foresight = Catalyst, Analysis, and Assessments.** Internal auditing is a catalyst for improving an organization's efficiency by providing insight and advice based on analysis and assessment of data and business process. Foresight illuminates potential future threats, or risks, if critical actions are not taken, and is a critical — if not *the* critical — element of value. Successful organizations are able to navigate tomorrow's often rapidly emerging risks, not simply relive yesterday's.
>
> **Objectivity = Integrity, Accountability, and Independence.** With commitment to integrity and accountability, internal auditing provides value to governing bodies and senior management as an objective source of advice enabled by internal audit's independence.[10]

Applying sound, fundamental internal auditing practices to help the organization achieve its strategic, operational, financial, and compliance objectives (assurance) is virtually synonymous with the benefits of general business acumen. The key value internal audit adds is its objective and independent assessment. As agents of change, we must make certain that we possess the business acumen to not just understand the organization's needs but to consistently demonstrate to our stakeholders how our business acumen, working in concert with independent, objective assurance, adds value. This addresses two of the three elements of the value proposition.

The final piece — insight and foresight — opens the door to not only enhancing that value but also to driving change. If we examine two critical components of insight and foresight, it is easy to make the case for internal audit driving change. Insight includes internal audit acting as a *catalyst for improving an organization's efficiency and effectiveness*. Foresight adds the dimension of internal audit illuminating *potential future threats, or risks, if critical actions are not taken, and rewarding opportunities if crucial actions are taken*. It is not a far stretch to conclude that internal audit can be *a catalyst for not only avoiding threats but also for pursuing opportunities*. That describes the agent of change value proposition.

In the past, I used a 2-by-2 matrix to illustrate the essential qualifications of a trusted advisor.

Exhibit 8-5 shows that being a trusted advisor is a function of at least two broadly framed capabilities that CAEs must possess: 1) risk, control, and governance expertise, and 2) strong relationship acumen.

It's time that I update that matrix to reflect the added components that lead to becoming an agent of change (see **exhibit 8-6**).

Exhibit 8-5
Ascending to the Level of Trusted Advisor

Relationship Acumen		
	A Good Lunch Partner	A Trusted Advisor with a Seat at the Table
	Taking Up Space	A Well-Kept Secret

Risk, Control & Governance Expertise

Exhibit 8-6
Ascending to the Level of Agent of Change

Relationship Acumen	A Good Lunch Partner	A True Agent of Change
	A Talking Head	A Trusted Advisor with a Seat at the Table
	Taking Up Space	A Well-Kept Secret

Risk, Control & Governance Expertise

One of the simplest definitions of change is *to make or become different*. Agents of change do both by becoming something different as they grow from being trusted advisors and by making their organizations different and better.

Chapter 9

The Strategic Internal Auditor

*If you don't know where you are going,
any road will take you there.*

— Lewis Carroll —

As a young internal auditor, I concentrated all of my energies on learning the audit standards and how to deliver sound internal engagements that were well planned, conducted, and reported. I had no time for abstracts such as "strategy." The word never even came up in my internal audit department. Eventually, I became a chief audit executive (CAE) and all of that changed. I began to understand why my predecessors had failed to win and sustain the support of internal audit's key stakeholders. They were focused on leading tactically sound internal audit functions, but they were never really focused more than a year ahead in leading the organization.

I began to contemplate what it would take for the internal audit function I had been selected to lead to deliver value and engender the support of stakeholders to make a greater investment in our department. I was formulating and executing a strategy without even realizing it. Then, almost three years after I was tapped to lead the internal audit department, something happened that fundamentally changed the way I saw the world. I was selected as one of only six civilians to attend the U.S. Army War College in Pennsylvania.

The name "War College" is a bit misleading. It is not an institution that teaches fighting wars or how to successfully deploy tactics in battle. On the contrary, the mission of the War College is "to educate and develop leaders for service at the strategic level." My year of residence at the institution helped equip me for a lifetime of serving subsequent roles with a strategic mindset. To any extent I ever became an "agent of change" in the organizations in which I later served, I attribute much of my success to the strategic mindset instilled in me at the U.S. Army War College.

While there, I learned to apply the principles of strategic thinking to how the Army was treating its internal audit resources. I wrote two or three papers that focused on the ramifications of downsizing the military's internal audit force, which I referenced in chapter 5. One of the papers was titled "Pay Now, and Pay Later." My message was simple: The Army was not being strategic by divesting itself of audit resources to address immediate budget reductions. Indeed, doing so eliminated the very tool it needed to identify cost reductions and savings opportunities necessitated by budget reductions. The situation was similar to that of a farmer who eats his seed corn to survive the winter. If you eat the seed corn, you will have nothing to plant later. It was the beginning of my infatuation with strategic thinking and internal audit.

The quote at the beginning of this chapter is a powerful one because it speaks a fundamental truth about strategy. *If you don't know where you are going, any road will take you there.* In other words, if there is no strategy, any solution will do.

Being Strategic Starts at Home

Before internal auditors can leverage a strategic mindset to be change agents within their organizations, they must be strategic in the way they drive change in internal audit itself. As a CAE, I have led every one of my audit departments through a strategic planning process almost immediately upon my appointment to the post. I view strategic plans like a roadmap, with a clearly marked destination (vision). Just as you should never embark on an extended road journey without GPS, I believe you should never undertake leadership of an internal audit department without a strategic plan.

It should come as no surprise then, that I was very pleased to see that the new Global Internal Audit Standards incorporate a mandate for strategic planning.

Principle 9 — *Plan Strategically* states:

> "The chief audit executive plans strategically to position the internal audit function to fulfill its mandate and achieve long-term success.
>
> Planning strategically requires the chief audit executive to understand the internal audit mandate and the organization's governance, risk management, and control processes. The internal audit function is resourced and positioned to support the organization's success through its strategy. In addition, the chief audit executive creates and implements methodologies to guide the internal audit function and develop the internal audit plan."

Further, Standard 9.2 — *Internal Audit Strategy* requires:

> "The chief audit executive must develop and implement a strategy for the internal audit function that supports the strategic objectives and success of the organization and aligns with the expectations of the board, senior management, and other key stakeholders.
>
> An internal audit strategy is a plan of action designed to achieve a long-term or overall objective. The internal audit strategy must include a vision, strategic objectives, and supporting initiatives for the internal audit function. An internal audit strategy helps guide the internal audit function toward the fulfillment of the internal audit mandate.
>
> The chief audit executive must review the internal audit strategy with the board and senior management periodically."[1]

I have always taken a classical view of strategic planning, believing that a sound plan should chart a vision three to five years into the future. It also must clearly outline how the internal audit department will bridge the gap from the present state to an envisioned future state. Whether leading strategic plans of my own departments or advising CAEs who were undertaking their own planning efforts, I have subscribed to essentially the same strategic planning process:

- **Identify/validate internal audit's key stakeholders.** For a first-time effort at developing a strategic plan, it is essential to identify internal audit's stakeholders. This will typically include the board, management, and regulators (in some industries). During subsequent updates to the strategic plan, it is always advisable to revalidate the list of key stakeholders.

- **Articulate the needs and expectations of internal audit stakeholders.** Understanding the needs and expectations of internal audit's stakeholders is vital to ultimately determining the vision. This phase will typically include interviews and conversations with critical members of the stakeholder groups, when possible. It is also important to focus on the needs and expectations they have for internal audit in five years, not just in the present.

- **Undertake a SWOT analysis.** Brainstorming sessions with the strategic planning taskforce should be used to identify internal audit's strengths, weaknesses, opportunities, and threats. That can be helpful in an eventual gap analysis.

- **Identify critical assumptions about the future.** Focus on those external forces that are and are not controllable. Assumptions can include forecasts or trends, such as those that are economic, regulatory, environmental, or industry.

- **Forge a vision.** Once stakeholder needs, SWOT analysis, and critical assumptions are formulated, it is time to articulate the vision. The vision should be succinct and aspirational. At the conclusion of our strategic planning process at TVA's Office of Inspector General, we articulated a vision of "Illuminating today's challenges and tomorrow's opportunities." The vision should also align with the strategy of the enterprise. If your company is planning to expand globally in the next five years, your strategic plan should clearly align.

- **Undertake a gap analysis.** Once the vision is articulated, it's time to compare where you are with where you need to be. It is the gap analysis that enables the formulation of the goals and objectives that make up the heart of the strategic plan.

- **Articulate strategic objectives.** Objectives will guide the internal audit department in the ultimate achievement of the strategic vision. Strategic objectives should articulate the desired outcome of the efforts that need to be undertaken. I have always preferred to limit the number of objectives, and have focused on those things that have to be corrected/accomplished to bridge the gap and enable achievement of the strategic vision. For each strategic objective, there should be three to five supporting initiatives. A supporting initiative should be a measurable step needed to achieve the objective. I typically refresh supporting initiatives as progress is achieved toward an objective.

The process I have outlined is the one I prefer to use; you may prefer an alternative approach. But by all means, have a strategic plan. We will never be change agents in our organizations if we are not willing to commit to strategic change within the internal audit function itself.

Exhibit 9-1 below provides a useful flow chart approach to visualize how an internal audit strategic plan can come together:

Exhibit 9-1
Blueprint for Developing a Strategic Plan

```
┌──────────────┐    ┌──────────────┐    ┌──────────────┐
│ Revalidate   │ →  │ Revalidate   │    │ Define Internal│
│ Stakeholders │    │ Stakeholder  │    │ Audit's Values │
│              │    │ Needs        │    │                │
└──────────────┘    └──────┬───────┘    └──────┬─────────┘
                           │                    │
                           ▼                    ▼
┌──────────────┐         ╔═══════════╗    ┌──────────────┐
│ Articulate   │         ║     A     ║    │ Identify Trends│
│ Internal     │    →    ║ Strategic ║ ←  │ and            │
│ Audit's      │         ║  Vision   ║    │ Assumptions    │
│ Mission      │         ╚═════╦═════╝    └──────────────┘
└──────────────┘               │
                               ▼
┌──────────────┐    ┌──────────────┐    ┌──────────────┐
│Develop       │    │Develop       │    │Critical      │
│Objectives    │ →  │Objectives    │ →  │Success       │
│to Achieve the│    │to Achieve the│    │Factors to    │
│Mission       │    │Objectives    │    │Monitor the   │
│              │    │              │    │Progress      │
└──────────────┘    └──────────────┘    └──────────────┘
```

Attributes of Strategic Internal Auditors

Strategic internal auditors are certainly capable of developing a strategic plan for internal audit. But not everyone who crafts a strategic plan is a strategic internal auditor. So, what does it take for an internal auditor to be truly strategic and be seen as strategic by management and the board? That was touched on in a valuable edition of The IIA's *Global Perspectives and Insights* series, "Elevating Internal Audit's Strategic Impact:"

Internal audit is uniquely positioned to be a strategic partner. With reporting relationships to the chief executive officer (CEO) or other executive officer, audit committee, and the board, high-performing CAEs combine intelligence, expertise, diligence, and curiosity in a manner that positions internal audit for a critical strategic role. Despite this, CAEs are not generally recognized for the potential strategic impact that they can have on their organizations. For CAEs looking to elevate the strategic role of internal audit, several questions should be answered to take this next logical and desired step. Does the CAE understand the strategic mission of the organization at a deep level? Does the CAE understand the perspective of the CEO and board and make the effort to become a trusted partner, offering advice and solutions that address key problems? Is internal audit aligned with the strategic mission? Is internal audit anticipatory and proactive (rather than reactive)? Does the CAE provide assurance on risk management?[2]

As The IIA emphasizes, strategic internal auditors combine intelligence, expertise, diligence, and curiosity in exercising a strategic role in the organization. But is this the full inventory of characteristics that a strategic auditor must possess? A *Forbes* article by Paloma Cantero-Gomez on the critical skills of successful strategic thinkers offers even more insight into what it takes. I believe the list is particularly appropriate when assessing the strategic acumen of internal auditors:[3]

Vision. According to Cantero-Gomez, "strategic thinkers are able to create and stick to a very clear visioning process." That is certainly true of internal auditors. As we discussed earlier, the ability to be visionary should begin with the vision for internal audit itself. Leaders in this profession have throughout its history been instrumental in crafting a future vision that enabled the profession to advance. Cantero-Gomez notes, "a clear, positive, and big enough vision is what inspires for action and pulls in ideas, people, and other resources." For internal auditors to be change agents, they must clearly grasp the vision of their enterprise, and bring their own strategic skills to bear on how change can facilitate achievement of the vision of the enterprise. They are not content to simply "count the beans," or even to advise on how the beans should be grown. Strategic internal auditors may well offer advice on whether beans are the right crop to grow.[4]

Framework. Cantero-Gomez builds on the need for vision by pointing out that "vision should be carefully embedded within a framework. Successful strategic thinkers have the ability to define their objectives and develop an action plan with goals broken down into tasks specifically measured in terms of timeline and resources." This is where internal auditors can leverage their natural strengths in left- brain thinking (logic) with right-brain thinking (creative), which are integral to strategic visioning and action. Strategic thinkers are self-aware and, as Cantero-Gomez puts it, "they are conscious of their own biases and factor their own circumstances, perspectives, and points of view within this framework."[5]

Perceptiveness. In its assessment of critical strategic thinking skills, Cantero-Gomez notes that "strategic thinkers are able to look around and understand the world from all different perspectives. They listen, hear, and read between the lines." This is a particularly important skill for the strategic internal auditor. Objectivity is a vital trait for our profession. If we undertake audits with preconceived biases, we do a disservice to those we audit and the enterprise as a whole. We complement that objectivity with keen perceptiveness and leverage creative thinking and intellectual curiosity in identifying causes and formulating solutions and future strategies. To be effective change agents, internal auditors must be keenly perceptive in identifying opportunities, not only for corrective measures, but for value creation through transformational change.[6]

Assertiveness. Strategic internal auditors are confident enough in their skills and abilities to be assertive when needed in promoting change. As Cantero-Gomez notes, "after a comprehensive evaluation, (strategic thinkers) choose the way to go and walk firmly into it with- out vacillation. They may doubt, but they do not let the doubts fog the vision. They communicate effectively what they want and need by using clear orders while simultaneously respecting the thoughts and wishes of others." Internal auditors don't "give orders," but those who are trusted advisors certainly command attention when they offer recommendations and advice. Assertiveness in the strategic internal auditor is most frequently demonstrated by persistence. If at first the strategic auditor doesn't succeed, they try and try again.[7]

Flexibility. One of the nine characteristics of outstanding internal auditors featured in *Trusted Advisors* was "open mindedness." I observed that "the truly outstanding internal auditors I have known thrive on change. They enthusiastically seek out opportunities to make quantum improvements in their approaches to audit and the solutions they identify when their audits identify risk management or control deficiencies."[8] Another word for the attribute I was describing is "flexibility," which happens to be one of the seven critical skills of strategic thinkers noted in the *Forbes* article. As Cantero-Gomez points out, "strategic thinkers are clearly aware of their weaknesses, so they are committed to seeking the advice of others. They are humble enough to be flexible and twist their ideas and framework as to truly achieve the desired vision. They do not confuse flexibility with lack of structure. They accept the rules of the game, because they are aware that, without rules, there is no fair game." Nothing could more aptly describe the open-minded internal auditor. Strategic internal auditors recognize that there are multiple paths to the same outcome and are more interested in the results that change will bring than in being right about how that change must be implemented.[9]

Emotional balance. In the words of Cantero-Gomez, strategic internal auditors "are able to balance their emotions in a way that always favors the achievement of the ultimate goals." The finest internal auditors I have ever known have been even-keeled, and did not let their emotions impair their sound judgment. As Cantero-Gomez puts it, "whether they received positive or negative feedback, they [strategic thinkers] are able to deal with it, understand, and respond in a way that protects and progresses toward their desired outcome." It is the ability to contain emotions that often differentiates good internal auditors from those who are truly great at their craft. During my career, I have faced intense pushback from those whose areas of responsibility may have been criticized in my audits. But I learned from some of my earliest mentors in the profession that emotional responses to strong negative reactions from management rarely resolve disputes. Strategic internal auditors recognize that success is attained only if positive beneficial change results from their work. Acrimonious disputes with those whom they trying to persuade will most likely end in failure.[10]

Patience. The seventh of the critical skills that strategic internal auditors must embrace is patience. As Cantero-Gomez notes, "strategic thinkers do not ignore that achievement is a long-term ride. Milestones all have a concrete time and moment. And success is the result of a process of strategically planned work and efforts. Strategic thinkers have the ability to be patient." Truer words could not be written about strategic internal auditors; they recognize that achievement of a vision is a long-term proposition. They also realize that change is the means by which strategic visions will ultimately be realized, and that patience will truly be a virtue if they are to be an agent of change. In the words of Leo Tolstoy: "The two most powerful warriors are patience and time."[11]

Avoiding the Pitfalls of Being a Tactical Internal Auditor

We are taught from the outset of our careers the importance of being "systematic and disciplined." Indeed, it remains as part of the definition of internal auditing in the Global Internal Audit Standards.

So, we become tactically focused on process that is often dictated by policies and procedures. We meticulously plan our engagements and document them in an audit program, which is often a step-by-step guide to undertaking the internal audit. We undertake the audit by gathering and tediously documenting the evidence necessary to draw conclusions. Finally, we prepare exhaustive reports that chronicle the results of our audits, which are then presented to those who are responsible for implementing corrective measures. We repeatedly undertake this process until many of us execute our roles with robotic precision. We become master tacticians in executing internal audits. Yet, to be agents of change, we must be anything but tactical. It is for this reason that the strategic internal auditor must avoid the pitfalls of being a tactician.

A few years ago, the Brainzooming Group published a short article highlighting six characteristics of strategic thinking skills as compared with tactical thinking. A review of this list highlights hurdles that classically trained internal auditors must overcome in their quest to be strategic internal auditors:

1. **A tactical thinker keeps opportunities and issues separate so that they are digestible.** The strategic internal auditor recognizes that the solution may not be to simply correct a problem. It may instead present an opportunity for the organization to take a completely different approach — one that will enhance value through greater efficiencies and effectiveness than could be achieved by simply correcting something that is broken.

2. **A tactical thinker looks at what is happening at face value.** A strategic internal auditor recognizes that the root cause may be far more complex than is evident on the surface. As I noted in *Trusted Advisors*: "Getting to the bottom of things requires more than just incessantly asking "why," as a child might do. If we did that, our clients would undoubtedly lose patience with us in short order, and our reputation for credibility would suffer." Strategic internal auditors do more than ask why. They exhibit strong critical thinking skills — "the ability to take information or a set of circumstances, consider the inherent challenges or weaknesses, identify deviation from acceptable criteria, and then do a root cause analysis to fully understand why something did or didn't happen."[12] That process often takes us to a very different conclusion than what might appear on the surface.

3. **A tactical thinker works to fill information holes, answering one question and moving to the next without asking any other questions in between.** The strategic internal auditor doesn't wait until an audit engagement is complete before applying critical thinking skills. They recognize that analyzing the results continuously may influence the next steps in evaluating a problem and will likely yield more timely insights.

4. **A tactical thinker is focused on checking items off a list to get it finished.** A strategic internal auditor recognizes that, to reach the strongest results, audit plans should remain dynamic. That kind of tactical thinking is a primary target of agile auditing, as discussed in chapter 5.

5. **A tactical thinker is sequential, focusing on one thing followed by another.** A strategic internal auditor recognizes that sequential thinking may limit their ability to observe the interconnected nature of systems and processes. It is only through a holistic examination of operations that transformational change can be envisioned and advised.

6. **A tactical thinker avoids complexity.** The strategic internal auditor embraces complexity, seeks solutions to challenges, and envisions opportunities to simplify complexity.[13]

It should be noted that tactical skills are still important when undertaking the internal audit mission. As Brainzooming notes, "The strongest businesspeople deliver on both strategy and tactics to create results."[14] However, strategic internal auditors recognize that tactical skills are simply enablers. They are important in undertaking the analysis that will ultimately enable the strategic mindset to formulate solutions that drive transformational change within the organization.

Strategic Internal Auditors and Transformational Change

Much has been written about transformational change. Simply defined, it is significant change designed to create "breakthrough value" for the organization. As Deloitte describes it, transformational change "involves strategic decisions that affect where you'll grow, how your organization operates, and what kinds of performance improvements you can expect."[15]

Given the profound nature of transformational change, is it reasonable to expect that internal auditors would be involved? I believe the answer must be an emphatic "yes!" While internal auditors certainly should not be the architects for such change, it is entirely reasonable to expect that they can be part of the process. If management and the board identify transformational change as a strategic goal of the enterprise, there will surely be risks and opportunities that should be identified and managed as part of the enterprise risk management system. Internal audit should ensure that associated risks are identified and included in its audit plan, as appropriate. More importantly, however, internal audit should be a strategic partner with management in seeking opportunities to drive transformational change.

Our contributions can come from insights on risks and controls and foresight on transformational opportunities. By leveraging the critical strategic thinking skills outlined in this chapter, internal auditors can leverage their seat at the table to be a strong advocate for change based on their knowledge of the business and their insights on the effectiveness of the organization's risk management, control, and governance processes.

Deloitte identified "six keys to unlocking breakthrough value in transformational change." I quote the opening section of each, and internal auditors would do well to remember and embrace them as they seek to be champions of transformational change:

1. **Begin with a strategy-informed ambition.** Leaders in business transformation typically have a clearly articulated, well-understood business strategy. Often an organization's strategic choices — although understood tacitly by senior leadership — are poorly translated into downstream implementation choices. The result? The dilution of value.

2. **Lead with capabilities.** Leaders in business transformation quickly focus and define the specific enterprise capabilities that will help achieve competitive advantage. In reality, only a small number of an organization's total capabilities play a critical role in helping the organization find new ways to differentiate and compete. Focusing on those critical capabilities can help deliver greater value, help leaders drive competitive advantage, and help the organization realize its business transformation ambition.

3. **Drive to value.** Leaders in business transformation articulate up front the value they expect to achieve through transformation, and they zealously monitor, measure, and track value throughout their transformation. Value should be the thread that links your business strategy and your transformation together. Take time to be explicit about exactly how you intend to create value. Then establish strong, clear connections to your execution plans.

4. **Build in sustainability.** Leaders in business transformation know that real value emerges over time through sustainable change that endures. To put the right capabilities, competencies, and change-adaptive culture in place for sustaining and growing the value of the transformation, data is essential. Leaders should use data-driven change management solutions. Such solutions should support a quantifiable, analytical approach to managing attitudes, behaviors, and engagement. And they should be more than generic solutions that fail to address the unique challenges of the organization.

5. **Be agile and flexible.** Leaders today should be prepared to continuously evolve through transformation because the business and technology landscapes in which they operate are continuously evolving. Leaders should work hard to embed agility, innovation, and a disruptive mindset into every transformation initiative.

6. **Invest in program talent.** Leaders in business transformation recognize that the right leader and right talent will make or break the success of the transformation. A strong program leader should have influence and credibility within the organization to make major shifts and shape how work gets done. Assigning a respected and capable business leader is critical to establishing the credibility and importance of the transformation to the organization's strategic goals.[16]

Obviously, not all change that internal auditors influence in their organizations will be transformational change. In fact, virtually every audit or advisory engagement should result in some change — even if it is only corrective in nature. However, the more transformational the change, the more a strategic mindset will benefit the internal auditor. As we will explore in chapter 11, an innovative mindset will also be a valuable asset for the internal auditor who contributes to the organization's transformational change initiatives.

Chapter 10

On Being Relationship Centric

Change before you have to.

— Jack Welch —

Persuading others requires a genuine level of trust. "You are just an internal auditor. Why should I listen to you when it comes to making a fundamental or critical change to my business?" Those we are trying to influence may not openly say that, but from my experience, it is certainly a barrier when we are trying to promote change. For that reason, it was not surprising to me that the CAE survey conducted for *Agents of Change* ranked relationship builder (66%) and dynamic communicator (44%) as the third and sixth most important attributes that an internal auditor must demonstrate to be an agent of change. Without those skills, we are stuck.

In chapter 8, I touched on how having solid business acumen supports the change agent's ability to communicate with stakeholders at their level. But that assumes a thorough understanding of the basic skills for relationship building in the workplace. Understanding how relationships are built and nurtured goes well beyond simply having a bubbly personality or an outgoing nature. I delve into that later in this chapter, but let's begin by addressing the benefits of building relationships.

There's significant research into the value of workplace relationships. Positive social interaction among co-workers is linked to mental and physical wellbeing. The opposite is true for social isolation. Researcher Elaine Houston, writing for *PositivePsychology.com*, explains this nicely: "Psychologists have long identified the desire to feel connected to others as a basic human need, with interpersonal relationships having a significant impact on mental health, health behavior, physical health, and mortality risk (Umberson & Montez, 2010). Indeed, human physiological systems are highly responsive to positive social interactions."[1]

Houston's article goes on to cite research linking close relationships to protecting against the adverse effects of stress (Gable & Gosnell, 2011); social pain in the workplace to actual physical pain (Dunbar & Dunbar, 1998); cooperative, trusting, and fair workplace relationships triggering the brain's reward center (Geue, 2017); and positive social interactions boosting physiological resourcefulness (Heaphy & Dutton, 2008).[2]

Foundational skills for building strong relationships are well established, and for many, those skills are instinctive or commonsensical. However, others struggle even to achieve these basic skills without a focused effort. I won't dwell too long in this area because agents of change are assumed to have mastered the basics of relationship building, but I offer the following primer for those just beginning or early in their careers. The modified list below is taken from an article in *Indeed.com*, but they are commonly understood as the building blocks of positive relationships.

> **Verbal communication skills.** Verbal communication is essential to building strong relationships. Finding opportunities to contribute ideas and ask questions shows you are interested and open to hearing the ideas of others as well as motivated to contribute.
>
> **Nonverbal communication skills.** Nonverbal communication also can have an impact on how you build relationships with others. For instance, learning how to read body language can help you pick up on other people's emotions. Understanding and being conscious of your own body language and the signals you put out are just as important.
>
> **Listening skills.** Active listening is an essential part of communication. It includes making eye contact, being aware of nonverbal cues, and asking questions that show you are invested in the conversation. This not only

shows that you respect the ideas of others, but it also indicates you care about all perspectives.

Networking skills. Meeting new people, exchanging ideas with other professionals, and offering assistance to other business professionals can help boost your networking skills. Effective networking skills increase professional reach and help form lasting professional relationships.

Team-building skills. Working as part of a team will almost always require effective relationship building. Develop your teamwork skills by practicing effective communication, showing respect for the ideas of others, and contributing and assisting where needed.

Empathy. Having empathy means you try to understand the feelings and emotions of others. Importantly, it involves experiencing another person's point of view, rather than just your own. Actively practicing empathy in the workplace signals to co-workers and managers your dedication to the overall success of the organization.

Emotional intelligence. Emotional intelligence combines several of the skills already discussed. It is the capacity to be aware of, control, and express one's emotions, and to handle interpersonal relationships judiciously and empathetically. Being emotionally intelligent means that you observe the dynamics in the workplace and find ways to contribute, help solve conflict, and generally work from a place of understanding.[3]

Before moving on, we should recognize that several of the basic skills outlined here are what I have been promoting for years in an internal audit context. Active listening and nonverbal communications should be part of the internal auditor's toolkit. Empathy and emotional intelligence also are vital in maintaining objectivity.

In my seminar, *Being an Agent of Change*, I share additional insights into the value of emotional intelligence. Goleman's Emotional Intelligence Model, developed by American psychologist and author Daniel Goleman, describes emotional intelligence as, "the ability to recognize, understand, and manage emotions in ourselves and others." The model is divided into four elements:

- Self-Awareness
- Self-Management

- Social Awareness
- Relationship Management

According to Goleman's studies, emotional intelligence contributes 80% to 90% of the competencies that distinguish outstanding leaders from average leaders.[4]

What's more, in *The Speed of Risk*, I address how to leverage basic relationship building to support continuous assessment of risk through a practice I call "shoe-leather assessments."

> "Another way to keep your risk assessment and audit plan up to date is what I like to call "risk assessment by walking around." This method is exactly as the phrase implies and relies on developing strong working relationships with key members of senior management. This way you know about new risks as soon as they do. Risk assessment by walking around may lack the discipline and structure of more formal assessments, but it's a powerful strategy for keeping in touch with what's happening in your organization and may reveal new risks that your formal risk indicators do not. Given the number of business units and executives in large companies, risk assessment by walking around cannot be the responsibility of only the CAE; the entire internal audit department must be organized and deployed."[5]

Even once mastered, basic relationship building must be raised to an even higher level. We must elevate our affiliations beyond appreciation and trust to a level of admiration and respect. This is where our relationships with our stakeholders must end up if we are to become change agents.

In *Trusted Advisors*, I dedicated a chapter to insightful relationships and covered several facets of how internal auditors can elevate connections with stakeholders. That included a reference to research I did with the Korn/Ferry Institute to examine personal attributes that maximize the impact of CAEs. That research identified six key relationship-building skills typically demonstrated by outstanding internal auditors:

Positive intent. It is critical for the client to see the internal auditor as fair, independent, and objective in their approach and as someone who has everyone's best interests at heart. Trusted advisors demonstrate a positive intent that makes it clear they aren't set on being right — but on finding the right answer.

Diplomacy. Trusted advisors are adept in direct, forthright communication (including listening) skills, political astuteness, and sensitivity to the organization's culture and how things get done. They are intuitive about people and have the ability to read an audience. They are masters at being contrarian without being confrontational.

Prescience. Identifying the risks ahead requires curiosity, an ability to see matters with fresh eyes, and a willingness to question assumptions. Trusted advisors can "see around corners." They anticipate the needs of clients before the needs are even evident, and they identify issues before they arise.

Trustworthiness. Trusted advisors walk the talk, keep confidences, operate with integrity, and are obsessive about maintaining credibility with clients. They are seen as professionals who can be counted on to repeatedly take the same course of action given the same set of circumstances time after time.

Leadership. Trusted advisors often set the tone for the entire internal audit staff. They are gifted at steering others toward consensus, managing conflict, and gaining alignment on issues.

Empathy. Trusted advisors understand and focus on each stakeholder's point of view, and they are sensitive to those needs and feelings. He or she must listen. A genuine caring about others amplifies all the other qualities on this list.[6]

Interestingly, empathy ranked high in the Korn/Ferry Institute research, just as it does in most discussions on basic relationship building. Indeed, several fundamentals of relationship building show up again and again on lists developed by leadership organizations when discussing change agents.

Novarete, the ethics arm of cloud-based data services provider XSInc., cites relationship building, which it calls being a "people person," as critical: "A Change Agent's strongest asset is their strong network with solid relationships, built on trust. These same healthy relationships build the open environment that fuels positive change and inspires Change Agents. If you are approachable and kind to others, and if you actively take care of your relationships, you are operating as a Change Agent. Remember, people do not want to grow if they do not trust the person pushing the change."[7]

Michigan State University includes effective listening skills: "Effective change agents are able to explore perspectives and take them into account when looking for solutions. This will help in getting buy-in to a change; people want to feel that others are listening to their ideas. Those who do will develop stronger relation- ships with their people by gaining trust."[8]

Change management consultant Enclaria addresses empathy: "Change agents must be able to put themselves in other people's shoes to understand their experience. You must predict how people will feel about change even if you don't feel that way. Empathy stops you from judging people for resisting change, so you can recognize that their response to change is normal and valid."[9]

I should note that much of the research on the qualities of change agents focuses on identifying individuals who can support planned change management within an organization. Change management typically describes approaches to prepare, support, and help individuals, teams, and organizations in making organizational change. But as noted in Michigan State University's course on Strategic Leadership and Management, "Whereas change management used to primarily focus on operational and/or process improvements and cost-effectiveness, it is now something that managers are using to think about how things get done regardless of institutional hierarchy."[10]

What's more, citing an article published in the *International Journal of Management, Business, and Administration*[11], Michigan State University notes, "the success of any change effort depends heavily on the quality and workability of the relationship between the change agent and the key decision-makers within the organization."

Adding to the Ranks of Change Agents

This provides an opportunity to revisit some of the data we examined in chapter 3 regarding how internal auditors see themselves.

Internal audit leaders overwhelmingly say they support the concept of acting as change agents. Yet, only 2 in 10 poll respondents (19%) view themselves as agents of change who partner with executive management to drive change that creates value. Nearly as many (15%) say they facilitate change, but it is up to management to drive change (see **exhibit 10-1**).

This data point indicates we have far to go as a profession. Recall that the same survey showed overwhelming support among respondents for internal auditors acting as change agents (90%). Respondents also believe they have support from stakeholders, reporting that 9 in 10 (90%) board members are moderately or fully supportive and more than 3 in 4 senior managers (76%) are, as well.

Exhibit 10-1
2 in 10 CAEs Operate as Agents of Change

Response	Percentage
Not sure	1%
None of the above	0%
I partner with executive management to drive change that creates value at every opportunity.	19%
I use both assurance and consulting to enhance value and advocate for change at every opportunity.	46%
I primarily use assurance to protect value and I use consulting to enhance value and advocate for change.	18%
I may facilitate change by identifying deficiencies, but management drives changes.	15%
My role in the organization is to protect value only (not drive change).	1%

Note: Q12 Which one of the following statements most closely reflects your view of yourself as an Agent of Change in your organization? n = 586

So, what is holding us back? I have addressed extensively the varied facets that feed a resistance to change. I believe there are two major contributors to why so many internal auditors appear to be willing but unable to join the ranks of change agents. Most internal auditors are reactive instead of proactive, and too many are caught in what I call the *independence trap*.

Reaching Beyond Trusted Advisor

As I have mentioned, much has been said and written about the value of building relationships to advance one's career. For internal auditors, the pinnacle is reaching the lofty level of trusted advisor to our stakeholders. A trusted advisor is someone who has earned a seat at the table, is viewed as a critical part of the team, and may even achieve the level articulated in The IIA's one-time 2030 vision statement and become "universally recognized as indispensable to effective governance, risk management, and control" within the organization.

However, as I have written throughout this book, internal auditors can no longer afford to be merely effective providers of assurance and advice. We must strive to become bold innovators for our organizations and drive positive change, especially in light of the growing speed of risk, expanding demands for effectively managing and leveraging risk, and the dire necessity to identify and anticipate emerging risks.

As noted in the discussion on the change agent value proposition (see chapter 8), change agents must strive to become catalysts for critical action. This requires becoming proactive. In other words, creating or controlling a situation by *causing something to happen* rather than responding to it afterwards.

Being proactive is a learned skill, and much has been written about the subject, primarily in addressing career development. Chrissy Scivicque, a Colorado-based career coach and corporate trainer, developed a five-step model for becoming proactive, which she published in her blog, *Eat Your Career*. In referring to the 5 P's model, she describes proactive people as "constantly moving forward, looking to the future, and making things happen. They're actively engaged, not passively observing. Being proactive is a way of thinking and acting."

This is the mindset that aspiring agents of change must embrace. Scivicque's 5 P's are:

> **Predict: In order to be proactive, you must first develop foresight.**
>
> Proactive people are rarely caught by surprise. Learn to anticipate problems and events. Understand how things work; look for patterns; recognize the regular routines, daily practices, and natural cycles that

exist in your business. At the same time, don't allow yourself to become complacent. Use your imagination when anticipating future outcomes. Don't simply expect the past to always be an accurate predictor for the future; use your creativity and logic. Come up with multiple scenarios for how events could unfold. Proactive people are always on their toes.

Prevent: Proactive people foresee potential obstacles and exert their power to find ways to overcome them before those obstacles turn into concrete roadblocks.

They prevent problems that others would simply look back on in hindsight and claim unavoidable. Don't allow yourself to get swept up in a feeling of powerlessness. When challenges approach, take control and confront them head on before they grow into overwhelming problems.

Plan: Proactive people plan for the future.

Avoid one-step, "here and now" thinking and instead, look ahead and anticipate long-term consequences. Bring the future into the present; what can you do today to ensure success tomorrow? Don't make decisions in a vacuum; every decision is a link in a chain of events leading to one final conclusion. In order to make the best decision, you have to know where you came from, where you are, and where you want to end up.

Participate: Proactive people are not idle observers; they are active participants.

In order to be proactive, you must get involved. You have to take initiative and be a part of the solution. Recognize that you are only a piece of the whole and that you influence — and are influenced by — the actions of others. Don't simply react to them. Engage with them. Exert your influence and make a contribution.

Perform: Being proactive means taking timely, effective action.

You must be decisive and willing to do the work NOW. Procrastination is not an option. Take ownership of your performance and hold yourself accountable. Stand behind your decisions. Being proactive means you have taken careful, thoughtful steps to choose the appropriate path; you're not just reacting impulsively to your environment.[12]

Each of those 5 P's can be applied readily to internal auditing. Indeed, many of them are synonymous with the skills of the best internal auditors. When proactive thinking is combined with the enterprisewide perspective, internal audit practitioners are in a powerful position to be catalysts for change.

By combining well-honed proactive skills with strong business acumen, internal auditors can accomplish great things. Having a keen understanding of gaps or deficits within the organization, gleaned from their assurance and advisory engagements, these agents of change are positioned to offer solutions that drive or create value. Internal auditors who excel as change agents are not afraid of revolutionary change. They are not timid. They speak up. If they see the potential to do something bold and decisive, they do it.

The Independence Trap

Throughout *Agents of Change*, I have referenced how the profession's focus on independence and objectivity can sometimes hinder advocacy for change. It doesn't have to. Agents of change are masters of the art of proactively driving change while maintaining independence and objectivity. Internal auditors striving to become change agents must become comfortable with this concept.

From early on, whether in university studies or early in our careers, internal auditors are indoctrinated to embrace and protect our independence and objectivity at all costs. Indeed, the heroes in our profession are those who muster the courage and integrity to battle those who would dare to tamper with them. Let me state clearly that I agree and wholeheartedly support this. Independence and objectivity are bedrock for providing effective internal audit assurance and advisory services that are critical to overall good governance.

But blind allegiance to those concepts can impede serving our organizations well. Admittedly, it is easier to accept and rigidly stick to simple constructs of complex concepts than to try to understand the details and nuances that drive them. However, the inherent danger in blind allegiance is that little in our professional or personal lives is a simple yes or no, good or bad, all or nothing. Agents of change must successfully deconstruct the details and nuances behind the profession's focus on independence and objectivity, and in doing so attain a greater understanding and appreciation of both.

Chapter 10: On Being Relationship Centric

Let's turn to the primary source of our connection to independence and objectivity — the *Standards*. The new Global Internal Audit Standards split discussions on independence and objectivity into separate domains, which was a long overdue fix, as we shall see.

Under the previous Standards, Standard 1100 – Independence and Objectivity, Standard 1120 – Individual Objectivity, and 1130 – Impairment to Independence or Objectivity addressed these critical areas. But treating them as one concept at best created confusion and at worse put up an unnecessary barrier toward progressing toward becoming agents of change.

Under the old Standard 1100 – Independence and Objectivity practitioners were told, "The internal audit activity must be independent, and internal auditors must be objective in performing their work."

If we break down the two concepts, we should first note that independence relates to the internal audit activity, and objectivity applies to individual internal auditors. In the context of practitioners acting as agents of change, this all but eliminates discussion of independence (don't worry, I will revisit the issue of independence later in this chapter).

Happily, the new Global Internal Audit Standards address these two vital areas in separate domains. Objectivity is addressed in Domain II, *Ethics and Professionalism*, and independence is addressed in Domain III, *Governing the Internal Audit Function*.

Let's take these two subjects one at a time. Objectivity is addressed in Principle 2 – *Maintain Objectivity* and standards 2.1 *Individual Objectivity* and 2.2 *Safeguarding Objectivity*. Let's look first at what the underlying principle addresses. Maintain Objectivity directs individual internal auditors to, "maintain an impartial and unbiased attitude when performing internal audit services and making decisions."[13]

Its focus is to ensure that internal auditors perform with the singular goal of producing work that is of the highest quality and not compromised by influences or factors that do not relate directly to the engagement. In addition, it makes the individual auditor's judgment the primary driver for that work.

The related standards, Standard 2.1 *Individual Objectivity* in part requires internal auditors to, "maintain professional objectivity when performing all aspects of internal audit services. Professional objectivity requires internal auditors to apply an impartial and unbiased mindset and make judgments based on balanced assessments of all relevant circumstances. Internal auditors must be aware of and manage potential biases."[14]

The final piece for purposes of this discussion is Standard 2.2 *Safeguarding Objectivity*. This standard in part directs internal auditors to, "recognize and avoid or mitigate actual, potential, and perceived impairments to objectivity. Internal auditors must not accept any tangible or intangible item, such as a gift, reward, or favor, that may impair or be presumed to impair objectivity. Internal auditors must avoid conflicts of interest and must not be unduly influenced by their own interests or the interests of others, including senior management or others in a position of authority, or by the political environment or other aspects of their surroundings."[15]

Importantly, the standard goes on to address when and how internal auditors must "recognize and avoid or mitigate actual, potential, and perceived impairments to objectivity." It also requires the CAE to establish methodologies to address impairments to objectivity and requires internal auditors to discuss impairments with the CAE or designee and take appropriate action.

Beyond the clear need to address conflicts of interest and avoiding the appearance of impairments to objectivity, Standard 2.2 – *Safeguarding Objectivity*, provides sound and specific guidance on what happens when an internal auditor must provide services in areas where they had previous responsibilities or previously provided advisory services.

This analysis of standards that address objectivity is designed to show that proactively working to support the organization's goals and strategies by acting as an Agent of Change need not jeopardize or compromise objectivity. Frankly, I have never believed that an objectivity impairment can occur unless and until an internal auditor is called upon to provide assurance on some aspect of work for which they were previously responsible.

I believe there is no objectivity impairment where we are providing advice or advocating for change, as long as we believe in our work product and no compromises are made in quality. The objectivity standards are primarily designed to protect the integrity of internal auditors' assurance work — not to prevent our engagement where the organization truly needs our expertise.

Independence Does Not Mean Isolation

I want to end this chapter by examining how the importance of internal audit independence was sometimes misconstrued to the detriment of the profession under the old Standards. We should first put internal audit independence in its proper perspective. Again, if we turn to the old *Standards* to begin the discussion, Standard 1100 – Independence and Objectivity stated simply that the internal audit activity must be independent.

The interpretation added clarity to this direction:

> *Independence is the freedom from conditions that threaten the ability of the internal audit activity to carry out internal audit responsibilities in an unbiased manner. To achieve the degree of independence necessary to effectively carry out the responsibilities of the internal audit activity, the chief audit executive has direct and unrestricted access to senior management and the board. This can be achieved through a dual-reporting relationship. Threats to independence must be managed at the individual auditor, engagement, functional, and organizational levels.*

Therefore, under the old Standards internal audit independence was tied primarily to three things: 1) freedom from conditions that threaten internal audit's unbiased assurance and advisory services, 2) direct and unrestricted access to senior management and the board, and 3) a recommended dual-reporting relationship.

The Global Internal Audit Standards address independence under Principle 7 — *Positioned Independently*. It is significant that this principle identifies as part of the board's responsibility "enabling the independence of the internal audit function. Independence is defined as the freedom from conditions that impair the ability of the internal audit function to carry out internal audit responsibilities in an unbiased manner."[16]

The relevant standard for this principle, Standard 7.1 *Organizational Independence* introduces new "essential conditions" that replace the idea of a dual-reporting relationship with the clear understanding at both the board and senior management level that the CAE reports directly to the board.

As noted earlier, under the old Standard 1130 – Impairment to Independence or Objectivity addressed how practitioners should alert stakeholders to impairment. There are genuine and serious threats to independence that can be created by scope limitations; restrictions on access to records, personnel, and properties; and resources limitations, such as funding. The requirement under 7.1 *Organizational Independence*, for CAEs to report annually to the board on the state of independence is a significant improvement in that it triggers a periodic review.

Over my career, I have witnessed and written about attempts by misguided or nefarious senior managers to control or limit internal audit by tightening the purse strings, manipulating its agenda, dictating its scope of work, blocking access to information or the board, and even physical intimidation. These are genuine and troubling examples of real threats to internal audit independence. The list of "essential conditions" introduced in the new Global Internal Audit Standards go a long way toward addressing potential threats to independence.

However, the answer to such threats is not to try to protect the function through separation and isolation. If anything, such defensive posturing makes internal audit only that much more mysterious, less understood, and undervalued.

Chapter 11

The Innovative Mindset

Innovation is the ability to see change as an opportunity, not a threat.

— Steve Jobs —

It is highly appropriate to begin a discussion about innovation with a quote from Steve Jobs, the late chairman, CEO, and co-founder of Apple Inc. The number of revolutionary inventions that have sprung from Apple's innovation hub in Cupertino, California, is truly astounding, especially considering they took place in a span of about 25 years.

From iPods to iPads, from iTunes to the Apple Watch, from the Macintosh personal computer to the ubiquitous iPhone, Apple's breakthroughs in computing, music, and entertainment are synonymous with these industries today. Indeed, the assembly line of invention from Apple has fundamentally changed the way we work, live, and play. The world lost one of the greatest innovators of the 20th century far too soon when Jobs succumbed to pancreatic cancer in 2011 at age 56. What he left behind is a company whose culture is steeped in innovation, and one that is the envy of the corporate world.

Of course, trying to replicate Apple's success by simply announcing, "We will be innovative starting today," is foolish. Jobs was able to instill an innovative mindset in his organization over time that was driven by his outsized personality and force of will. There have been numerous published accounts of his rudeness and outright cruelty to those he viewed as getting in the way of what he wanted. However, in the end, he succeeded in building an organization that thrives on change. Those who successfully innovate must embrace change, and those who seek to drive change must have an innovative spirit. To be sure, to innovate is to make changes in something established, especially by introducing new methods, ideas, or products. Therefore, agents of change must innovate. That is not to say they must possess innate skills to invent new, revolutionary products. Instead, they must have a deep and intuitive understanding of how change creates value.

Prepare Yourself for Innovation

Innovative thinking does not come naturally, especially for those of us in internal auditing. If you're not an innovator, don't feel bad; you are not alone. Traditional education systems focus on teaching through lecturing and learning by listening. They measure achievement in test scores rather than examination and debate. While such long-held, global teaching practices do not openly discourage innovation, they don't do much to nurture it. But what would happen if we began with a different proposition? What if we could unleash the potential of anyone to innovate?

That is precisely what Ami Dror did when he and his partners began a company called LeapLearner in Shanghai, which was featured in a *Forbes* article. The company taught children computer code and challenged them to create a video game. Dror's central premise was that the trial-and-error process of writing lines of code and testing them by hitting "execute" would help break down barriers to innovation. We can take three valuable lessons from LeapLearner's approach.

> **Free yourself from the fear of failure.** Coding allows for almost instantaneous feedback, which creates a comfort level with asking and receiving feedback and direction. It also helps with developing critical thinking and problem-solving skills, all while teaching children to innovate.
>
> **Create a culture where innovation is rewarded.** The LeapLearner process has a built-in reward. Successful innovation equals a cool new

video game. In addition, Dror encourages innovation as an employer by rewarding employees who take risks.

Make risk-taking a more consistent behavior. This concept may be anathema to many in a profession centered on managing risk, but it is critical to breaking away from traditional approaches that often dissuade asking for feedback and rewarding risk taking and "outside-the- box" thinking.

Dror received a significant affirmation for his approach to innovation just three years after opening the doors at LeapLearner. He was awarded China's prestigious Yicai Brilliant prize in 2018 as one of that nation's top entrepreneurs. Today, LeapLearner is the world's largest coding education company with clients in more than 20 countries."

My core innovation principles are very simple no matter if I share it with my students, my employees, or my kids," Dror told *Forbes*. "Have more dreams than achievements. Chase your dreams as fast as you can, and fail fast if needed, but always, always ask 'Why?'"[1]

Dror's final point should resonate with internal auditors. Every practitioner's toolbox must include that simple but powerful three-letter word — why.

In *Trusted Advisors*, I examined in depth 10 characteristics of outstanding internal auditors. These were the keys that helped elevate top performers in our profession to the vaunted level of trusted advisor. As I discussed in chapter 9, one of the characteristics was open-mindedness, which is particularly relevant to being innovative. In reviewing the chapter on open-mindedness, I was struck with how much it focused on being open to change and innovation. From *Trusted Advisors*:

> "Open-mindedness can be deeply challenged by change. Rather than simply being open to change and riding it out, outstanding internal auditors are typically agents of change. They create buy-in, motivate action, maintain momentum, and establish a sense of urgency even when management may have other priorities. If you believe, as I do, that internal audit can bring about positive change, you must embrace change not only in what you do but how you do it.
>
> This ties in with stakeholder expectations, which have shifted over time. Boards and audit committees now expect internal auditors to follow the

risks. So, when new risks emerge or old risks rear their ugly heads (and they do regularly), their expectations of us transform accordingly. As I noted in Lessons Learned on the Audit Trail, our stakeholders ultimately judge our value. I would also add that it is our stakeholders who will ultimately decide the extent to which we are trusted advisors.

Being open to change enables us to have a hand in choosing what we want change to look like. That is pretty powerful stuff, but it doesn't come without a significant threat — complacency. The minute we become complacent and think we know everything there is to know about internal auditing, the risks we audit, and feel we no longer need to invest in learning and growing, we cease to be an outstanding internal auditor or an agent of change. And we will certainly never step into or sustain the role of trusted advisor."[2]

In the same chapter, I shared some important experiences about practices and habits that can act against open-mindedness. It manifested itself in a list of things not to do, and should be on the wall of every internal auditor seeking to be a change agent:

Don't dwell on the past. How likely is it that people will seek your advice if you tell them only how things used to be done? They may find the information interesting from a strictly historical perspective, but ultimately, they need help knowing what to do right now, in six months, or next year. If you're not able to envision what the future looks like from your client's point of view, your client won't view you as a valuable resource. Over time we have seen many innovations that enable internal audit to adapt and maintain or become more valuable. Technology is a good example because it multiplies our capacity to an extraordinary degree. If we focus on old ways of conducting an audit, we will be unable to audit at the speed of risk and will quickly lose credibility and stature as a trusted resource.

Don't shrink from getting to the bottom of issues. You will always struggle to find the root cause of an issue if you are not open-minded. I have seen internal auditors arrive at the end of the audit process and still display a stunning lack of understanding of the issue. For example, they may report a condition (a failure in a control in a certain area) and an unsupported, under-researched cause (the people in that area are not adequately trained), then provide an underwhelming or painfully obvious recommendation (do a better job training). Well, that may look fine, albeit uninspiring, on the surface. But what if the cause that was articulated wasn't the true root cause of the control failure? Perhaps there was no reinforcement mechanism in place to drive employees to follow company policies. Or maybe culture was the culprit; possibly the prevailing corporate philosophy was one of the ends justifying the means, thereby excusing the lack of effective controls. The point is, if you are complacent and not open to digging deeper, you are unlikely to get to the root cause and, as a consequence, your value will be significantly diminished.

Don't take a myopic view in making recommendations. The easy solution may be right, but it also may not. In many instances, if the obvious solution was the right one, chances are that it would have already been conceived and implemented. It's best to assume there is a reason that solution isn't already in place; maybe it has been tried and abandoned because of a lack of success, or it wasn't assessed as a critical enough risk to even test the solution. Open-mindedness calls for creativity — being willing to explore alternative explanations for why something happened and proposing creative solutions for ensuring it doesn't happen again. Of course, there is some risk to this approach. Lars Christensen reminds us that there are people who will mistake internal audit's guidance or recommendation for creative solutions as "approval by the auditors" to do what they want. This should not cause us to abandon creativity, however; we simply have to be prepared to defend our recommendations with as much creativity as we used to develop them.

Don't neglect to seek input from those you are auditing. Internal auditors are often compared, rarely flatteringly, with police officers. So, let's imagine a police officer stops you for speeding and prepares to give you a ticket. You respond by suggesting that the two of you work together to find a different solution, rather than a ticket. While the officer would probably be disinclined to consider such an option, this is metaphorically what internal auditors must sometimes be willing to do in their audits.

One of the AEC survey respondents pointed out how critical this aspect of open-mindedness is to an activity in which internal auditors participate on a regular basis — negotiation. Effective negotiation means not automatically imposing your own solution when another may be just as good or better; it is based on an appreciation for what can be achieved if we are open to alternatives. We must be willing to hear our clients' views, discuss them, and work toward a mutually acceptable solution.

Don't view the world in black and white. There are often multiple paths to the same outcome. Outstanding internal auditors explore these paths, discuss their advantages and disadvantages, and assess their risk. An ability to navigate ambiguity was specifically called out by one of the AEC survey respondents who described it as "comfort and skill in dealing with competing truths." I like that particular definition because it seems especially pertinent to internal auditing. The ability to see beyond black and white ties in with a point I made on ethical resiliency in chapter 2 — the need to leave preconceived notions at the door. Never enter an audit with your findings, solutions, or opinion of the involved parties already in mind.

Learning to Innovate

What steps can we take to become more innovative? Mikael Eriksson Björling knows a thing or two about innovation, and he's passionate about it. Indeed, his title at the Ericsson Networked Society Lab is Networked Society *Evangelist*. Björling, whose work at the lab supports creation of "networked societies," believes most innovation is directly or indirectly driven by new technology. So, understanding new technology and its impact is an essential prerequisite to innovation.

Björling authored a series of blog posts for the Networked Society Lab about innovation that capture key steps to creating an innovative mindset.[4] I'll share an abbreviated version of those posts here and discuss how Björling's insights can be applied by agents of change within their organizations.

Be open to change. This concept has already been thoroughly discussed, but Björling adds an admonition to remain curious about the constant state of trans- formation by keeping track of change and new technology and constantly analyzing the real and potential consequences of transformative change. From an internal audit perspective, Björling's direction describes concisely how practitioners should view the way their organizations are embracing new technologies. Earlier, I concluded that internal auditors must "understand the business" of their organizations, but I could expand that to emphasize that internal auditors must "understand the business and the technology that enables value creation."

Embrace creativity. Björling makes the case that creativity replaces traditional scientific method in an innovative mindset. This argument is predominant among many who have successfully practiced innovation in the realm of daily business activities. This innovation-as-art approach — versus innovation as science — doesn't rule out the need for structure, process, and methodology. All are required for innovation. However, it begins with the premise that creativity rather than process is the starting point for innovation.

That may be particularly challenging for internal auditors. The very definition of the profession describes a "systematic, disciplined approach." However, a differentiator between those who are followers in our profession from those who are innovators may well be a creative mindset. We can certainly be technically sound and creative at the same time.

Think big. Innovation is more than just incremental improvements to existing products. Innovation requires the ability and courage to think beyond the normal or status quo. Björling argues that big thinking and innovation combine analytical skills, entrepreneurial spirit, and the ability to fantasize. I have already addressed the first two skills, but few associate fantasizing with work. Indeed, the very definition of fantasizing — to indulge in daydreaming about something desired — includes negative connotations associated with *indulging* and *daydreaming*.

It should not be surprising that internal auditors, whose processes are steeped in traditional scientific method, rarely nurture such behaviors as part of their professional development. Björling suggests big thinking is more easily achieved in diverse organizational cultures versus "homogenous groups that are likely to reproduce versions of similar thinking over and over again."[5]

Be courageous. Björling eloquently writes, "It takes courage not to conform to widespread beliefs and popular 'truths' in big organizations. It takes courage to challenge proven strategies and successful products and services before they go into decline. It takes courage to question management and colleagues for doing things the way they have always done. It takes courage to constantly problematize and be that one person who always goes against the grain and tries to think about things from a different angle. It takes courage to be vulnerable rather than playing it safe according to established business practice. It takes courage to venture into the new and uncertain, risking failure."

We often speak of the need for internal auditors to be courageous in executing their role. However, we are typically speaking of the courage to highlight what isn't working or what is wrong. Björling is speaking about the courage to identify what might be. While it can be intimidating and frightening, risk-taking is critical to innovation. Innovation doesn't happen when people *dare to be the same.*

Think and act fast. One of the most difficult aspects of change is overcoming the reluctance to act. Those with an innovative mindset learn not just to set that reluctance aside but to understand intuitively that innovation requires a fast-moving process to keep up with change. I speak extensively about auditing at the *speed of risk.* Change agents must *innovate at the speed of change.*

This is not an easy concept for most people to grasp. That's primarily because humans are linear thinkers and change driven by technology is moving at an exponential rate. I addressed the challenges of exponential thinking in an October 2019 blog post by quoting celebrated entrepreneur, innovator, and founder and chairman of the X Prize Foundation, Peter Diamandis. He addresses exponential change using a simple explanation:

30 linear steps @ 1 meter per step = 30 meters

30 exponential steps @ 1 meter (1, 2, 4, 8, 16, 32, 64, 128, etc.) =

1,073,741,824 meters

Björling notes that twentieth century innovation was typically a slow process, with product concepts going from the drawing board to the showroom in a span of years! With advanced technology in 3D printing and virtual reality-assisted design and manufacturing, that process has been shrunk to a matter of months or weeks. In addition to acting fast, Björling references the need to fail fast.

"In this context, it's also critical to adhere to the notion of 'failing fast,' as new ideas and concepts have to be tested out quickly and be shut down just as quickly if they don't fly. In this way, the organization can move resources to the next concept instead of getting stuck in a dead-end innovation project, because after all, the world's next 'big idea' is just around the corner."[6]

I believe this aspect of innovation is significant enough to merit its own step.

Fail fast, fail gracefully. Daniel Burrus, an innovation expert and futurist, notes that no matter the exponential speed of change and innovation, the statistical relationship between failure and innovation remains consistent. "Studies have shown it can take upward of 3,000 ideas to produce one product or service that goes on to be a commercial success. It is rare to capture lightning in a bottle instantaneously these days without that same rate of failure of the past."[7]

As with the LeapLearning teaching method, there's a value in failure if it leads to an eventual successful outcome. That is why failing fast is a must. "Failing fast allows you to move on from that missed shot much sooner so you can get to the next effort, which will yield better results," according to Burrus.[8]

As internal auditors, we are programmed to be averse to failure. So, embracing the idea that there is value in failure is a challenge for many in our profession. Yet, to be innovative change agents, we must accept that failure is a risk that comes with innovation and change. By understanding that failure is part and parcel to innovation, we also should refrain from seeking blame or pointing fingers when an innovative effort falls short.

I could devote entire chapters to each of the six topics covered in this section. To be sure, the art of innovation and creativity has launched the careers of countless inventors, psychologists, artists, not to mention art critics. These six elements provide a sound beginning to our investigation of innovation. As I mentioned earlier, it is foolish to think we can become innovative overnight. But, as with anything of value, an innovative mindset is something to strive for and a critical tool in the change agent's toolbox.

Why Innovation for Internal Audit?

Throughout *Agents of Change*, I have made the case that not only can internal audit drive positive change in the organization it serves, but internal audit itself must undergo a fundamental change to bring this about. As the demands grow on organizations to be more flexible and resilient in the face of accelerating technological disruption, opportunities and risk abound. Those who develop the skills to become agents of change will be the ones who not only identify and provide assurance on those risks, but also those who help their organizations exploit the opportunities.

The value of having change agents on the payroll is becoming increasingly evident. There is growing demand from the C-suite for informed, innovative ideas that support decisive and positive action and change.

A key finding from an IBM report published in the midst of the COVID-19 pandemic supports the premise. The report from the Institute for Business Value identified an evolution in thinking by senior management on how business would operate in a post-pandemic world. "Leaders are expecting more from their transformation initiatives. They identify competitiveness and workforce resilience as the benefits they most want from ongoing digital transformation."[9]

One of the senior management epiphanies identified in "COVID-19 and the Future of Business" was that "traumatic stress has hijacked corporate strategy."

> "Executives are tasked with defining their organizations' vision. But it can be hard to focus if they are continually putting out fires. While workforce safety and resilience, cost management, and organization agility emerge as top priorities for the short- and longer-term, the pandemic has amplified old business fears and introduced new ones. The result? Executives are enamored with the priority du jour."[10]

The acceleration of technology adoption, growing reliance on big data, the introduction of generative AI, and the near-universal acceptance of remote work for most industries have further fueled business strategies designed to thrive amid chaos.

If senior management is indeed hyper-focused on issues of the day, internal audit must be able to deliver the immediacy, resilience, agility, and innovation that will demand.

A Final Thought on Innovation

Being in an atmosphere where innovation, creativity, and change can thrive is incredibly fulfilling. Several times in my career I have found myself in such a position and was able to make real change. Throughout my professional life, I also have strived to be open to new opportunities, new adventures, and new perspectives. Like many others, I have a healthy respect for career opportunities with all their commensurate benefits. But I have always been driven by much more. When I grew weary in a position, I knew I was no longer learning or growing. I refused to be caught in a rut, and even left a higher-paying position simply because it was ceaselessly routine and mundane.

I frequently advise young internal auditors to not be afraid to move to another company, or even leave the profession for a while and return when recharged. If you lose the spark, energy, drive, or innovative mindset, your effectiveness as a change agent wanes.

Conclusion

Agents of the Future

There is nothing permanent except change.

— Heraclitus —

Over my long and gratifying career in internal auditing, I have witnessed great strides as the profession has repeatedly pivoted to react and adapt to each challenge that has come its way. The profession's journey is impressive and inspiring. We have gone from providing accounting-focused assurance over financial controls to offering assurance related to the full portfolio of risks by leveraging hindsight, insight, and foresight. Indeed, it could be argued that we have progressed from being mere "counters of change" to positioning ourselves as "agents of change."

Throughout this book, I examined internal auditing's evolution, from its origins to today's modern profession, and the arc of that history has indeed been much more evolution than revolution. That must change. We can no longer afford the comfort of only responding or reacting. We must be proactive. The forces that control modern business, economies, and societies demand agility and resilience, and our organizations deserve nothing less from us. Internal audit must be on the forefront of change.

Fueled by technology and disruption, the pace of transformation today is accelerating to a point of turmoil. Yet, throughout history, those two factors have been ever-present as catalysts for change. Familiar epochs driven by technological disruption are part of the lexicon of human achievement — the Bronze Age, the Renaissance, the Industrial Revolution, the Atomic Age, the Digital Age, the rapidly emerging age of AI.

We must take heart and inspiration from the times in which we live and rise to the challenges of a world undergoing exponential change.

Revolutionary Evolution

Beyond its context in government or military terms, the word *revolution* describes a dramatic and wide-reaching change in the way something works or is organized, or in people's ideas about it. In contrast, the word *evolution* is the gradual development of something, especially from a simple to a more complex form. While seemingly contradictory, the two concepts can be combined. *Revolutionary evolution* describes a dramatic and wide-reaching change to a more complex form. This is what is necessary for internal audit, and the leaders of this revolutionary evolution are the agents of change among us, as well as the agents of the future.

Agents of Change has addressed key aspects of what that revolutionary evolution must entail. They include:

- Transforming our mindsets to thrive in an era in which change is fast-paced, dynamic, and unrelenting.
- Acknowledging our shortcomings as a profession and as individual practitioners — and committing to improve them.
- Letting go of comfortable, outdated processes and accepting radical ways of thinking.
- Embracing technology in the way we undertake our mission and as a focus of our mission.
- Expanding our skillsets in communication, innovation, and proactive thinking.
- Viewing independence and objectivity as tools for change — not barriers.
- Willingly taking on the mantle of agents of change.

Throughout history, successful revolutionaries have been those who could inspire and enact radical change. The characteristics of those revolutionary leaders and the tactics they used to inspire change have been thoroughly examined. We can look to those studies to inspire our own revolutionary evolution. Inspiring Leadership Now, a leadership training organization, makes it its business to know and understand revolutionary thinking. It offers 10 ways to become a "powerful voice for change." By now, the items from that list — condensed below — should start to sound familiar.

1. **Use your voice and speak out.** Your voice is the spark to potentially ignite the fire of change.
2. **Take a step.** The biggest thing in starting a motion for change is taking the first step.
3. **Communication.** Articulate your vision. What do you want to accomplish and why?
4. **Tell the story.** Behind every movement for change there is a story. It's the story that enables others to rally around a common purpose.
5. **Be bold. Be innovative.** Movement starters are those who say, "There must be more that we can do."
6. **Use setbacks.** Leverage failures as learning opportunities, not as deal breakers.
7. **Gain skills as you go.** Start small and grow your skill base.
8. **Stay focused.** Make it your mission to hone your focus on what it is you want to see and build your determination through accepting the challenges that come your way.
9. **Generate and appreciate your followers.** If you are the spark for change, your supporters are the kindling for your fire. Encouraging and supporting your followers is key to generating momentum.
10. **Remember the big picture — and the little guys.** People care about purpose. Let this allow your movement to inspire change and gain momentum.[1]

Agents of Change Are Among Us

Throughout this book, I have shared the thoughts of several internal audit leaders who have embraced the change-agent attitude and leveraged it for success. Their observations and counsel about courage, innovation, communication, and relevance provide ample inspiration for applying the change agent mindset to our work as internal auditors. Importantly, we must realize that there are many would-be change agents who have yet to reach the highest levels, particularly those among the newest members of our profession.

An *Internal Auditor* magazine article on its 2020 class of "Emerging Leaders" eloquently described how that year's crop of young visionaries were already equipped with the change-agent mindset.

> "Emerging Leaders extol internal audit's access to all levels of an organization and its role in strategic planning. Even at relatively early stages in their careers, they're already earning seats at the proverbial table. And those seats are earned based on both their mastery of internal audit processes and their ability to see the bigger picture. As a result, they report leading massive international engagements, jumping into complicated situations on short notice, and starting up audit functions at far-flung branches of their organizations. Adeptness with data is a given with this group. No longer is data analytics a sought-after specialty — this year's class fiddles with numbers for fun, and many write software suited to their department's specific needs on technology and the requisite skills to support it."[2]

The 2023 descriptions of the magazine's "Emerging Leaders" further strengthened the concepts of innovation and change as fundamental to the next generation of internal audit leaders.

> "In the ever-shifting technology landscape, where generative AI and expansive language models have taken center stage, a bright horizon emerges for the internal audit profession. This year's 15 exceptional Emerging Leaders have not only embraced the winds of change but harnessed them to steer the course of innovation. Data analytics is a mainstay of their practice and their pragmatic approach to incorporating new tools in their operations showcases their adaptability and versatility. These Emerging Leaders embody a resounding beacon of optimism and are a testament to the internal audit profession's boundless potential for harnessing innovation, collaboration, and vision."[3]

Those descriptions of the young internal audit leaders (all 30 years old or younger) gives me great hope that the newest crop of internal auditors are keen to embrace the change-agent mindset and, in some ways, are better equipped to assume the mantle. This does not mean those who have worked in the profession for longer periods are unable to achieve such forward-looking greatness. However, they should look at their younger colleagues as potential mentors for guidance in leveraging technology, innovation, and process change.

Remaining True to the Profession

Our definition of revolutionary evolution describes "a dramatic and wide-reaching change to a more complex form." What it doesn't describe is abandoning or rewriting the fundamentals of the profession. What has made internal auditing one of the greatest professions — and one on the cusp of being even greater — are its core principles. Even as we strive to become agents of change, our focus and commitment to our core principles — integrity, competence, objectivity, alignment, quality, self-improvement, communications, insights, being proactive, and promoting improvement within the organizations we serve — must never waver. Indeed, following the core principles is part of the formula for success.

Successful agents of change understand that the change we promote and drive within our organizations must be enabled by our other work. Internal auditors exist to serve their organizations with assurance and advice, and only when we consistently provide those services at the highest levels can we become agents of change.

But don't confuse efficiency or adopting new processes with being change agents. It is not about finding new ways to generate a report. It is not about becoming an IT expert or learning to write code. It is not even about being the cleverest or the most innovative person in the room. It is about embracing a way of life that continuously seeks positive change. Change is not a process — it is an outcome.

The Constancy of Change

The quote from the Greek philosopher Heraclitus that opens this chapter provides a good close to this book and a good beginning to your journey as an agent of change. Change is constant, Heraclitus judged, change is the only thing that is permanent. He also is credited with the aphorism, "No man steps in the same river twice." This fits with his fundamental premise because the river and the man are constantly changing. Today the river is a raging torrent of change, and we as agents of change must help guide our organizations safely across it.

Go forth and be an agent of change!

Notes

Chapter 1: An Evolving Profession

1. B. Bernstein, *Against the Gods: The Remarkable Story of Risk* (New York, NY: John Wiley & Sons, Inc., 1996).
2. *2023 North American Pulse of Internal Audit: Bridging Critical Gaps* (Lake Mary, FL: The Institute of Internal Auditors, 2023).
3. Internal Audit: Vision 2035, The Institute of Internal Auditors, Lake Mary, FL, 2023.
4. "Amount of Data Created Daily (2024)," Duarte, F., Exploding Topics, Dec. 13, 2023.
5. *Seeing through walls to find new horizons*, PwC Global Internal Audit Study 2023, PwC, 2023.
6. 2023 Next Generation Internal Audit Survey, Protiviti, 2023.
7. *North American Pulse of Internal Audit: The Internal Audit Transformation Imperative*, The Institute of Internal Auditors, Lake Mary, FL, 2018.
8. *Agile Internal Audit: Leading practices on the journey to becoming Agile*, Global Knowledge Brief, The Institute of Internal Auditors, Lake Mary, FL, 2019

Chapter 2: Responding to Risk in Permacrisis

1. *A Year of Permacrisis*, Collins Language Lovers blog, Shariatmadari, D., Nov. 1, 2022, https://blog.collinsdictionary.com/language-lovers/a-year-of-permacrisis/
2. *Get There Early: Sensing the Future to Compete in the Present*, Johansen, B., San Francisco, CA: Berrett-Koehler Publishers, Inc. pp. 51–53. ISBN 978-1-57675-440-5, 2007.
3. *Strategic Management Simulations to Prepare for VUCAD Terrorism*, Satish, Usha and Siegfried Streufert, Journal of Homeland Security, June 2006.
4. *Facing the Age of Chaos*, Cascio, Jamaise, Medium.com, April 2020.
5. *The Black Swan: The Impact of the Highly Improbable (2nd ed.)*, Taleb, Nassim Nicholas, London: Penguin, 2010.
6. *Facing the Age of Chaos*, Cascio, Jamaise, Medium.com, April 2020.

Chapter 3: Independence Doesn't Imply Isolation

1. Timothy Berichon, *Ready and Relevant: Prepare to Audit What Matters Most* (Lake Mary, FL: Internal Audit Foundation, 2020).
2. Richard Branson, located and accessed on many sites, including pinterest.com, me.me, twitter, and quotestats.com.
3. S. Ramamoorti, *Internal Auditing: History, Evolution, and Prospects* (Lake Mary, FL: Internal Audit Foundation, 2003).
4. Ibid.
5. *Global Internal Audit Standards*, The Institute of Internal Auditors (2024).
6. Ibid.
7. Ibid.
8. Ibid.
9. E. Whiteacre Jr., http://www.brainyquote.com/quotes/quotes/e/edwardwhit516604.html

Chapter 4: Agent Change Thyself

1. E. D. Hirsch Jr., Joseph F. Kett, and James Trefil, eds. (2002). "Physician, heal thyself." *The New Dictionary of Cultural Literacy* (Boston: Houghton Mifflin).
2. Richard F. Chambers, (2024), "2024 Focus on the Future," AuditBoard, Cerritos, CA.
3. "2023 Next-Generation Internal Audit Survey," Protiviti, Menlo Park, CA, 2023.
4. Shaun Willcocks, et al, (2023), "Global Internal Audit Study 2023: Seeing through walls to find new horizons," PwC, London, UK
5. Shannon Urban, "The innovative internal auditor," *Internal Auditor* (June 2017): 49.
6. "Times Call for Liberal Action, Says Kennedy," Lodi (Calif.) *News-Sentinel*, May 13, 1961, 3.
7. Rosabeth Moss Kanter, "10 Reasons Why People Resist Change," *Harvard Business Review* (Sept. 25, 2012), https:/hbr.org/2012/09/ten-reasons-people-resist-change
8. "Agile Auditing: Transforming the Internal Audit Process," Executive Summary (Lake Mary, FL: Internal Audit Foundation, 2020), 4.
9. Ibid.
10. Global Internal Audit Standards, Domain V: Performing Internal Audit Services, (Lake Mary, FL: The Institute of Internal Auditors, 2024)
11. Ibid
12. Government Auditing Standards, 2018 Revision, U.S. Government Accountability Office, GAO-18-568G (Washington, D.C.: 2018), 191.
13. Shaun Willcocks, etal, (2023), "Global Internal Audit Study 2023: Seeing through walls to find new horizons," PwC, London, UK

14. "The Road Ahead for Internal Audit: 5 Bold Predictions for the 2020s," Chambers on the Profession, *Internal Auditor* (Nov. 4, 2019).

15. Global Internal Audit Standards, Domain I: Purpose of Internal Auditing, The Institute of Internal Auditors (2024).

16. "Leveraging an innovative internal audit strategy to sell your story of value," *Resilient* podcast (New York, NY: Deloitte, 2020).

Chapter 5: Driving Change

1. Richard F. Chambers, *The Speed of Risk: Lessons Learned on the Audit Trail*, 2nd Edition (Lake Mary, FL: Internal Audit Foundation, 2019), 22.
2. "What is Agile Auditing? The Benefits of Taking Your Audit Team Agile," AuditBoard.
3. Ibid.
4. "Becoming Agile: A guide to elevating internal audit's performance and value, Part 1: Understanding Agile Internal Audit," Deloitte.
5. Ibid.
6. Toby DeRoche, *Agile Audit Transformation and Beyond*, (Taylor & Francis Group, LLC, CRC Press, 2022).
7. Ibid.
8. Ibid.
9. Rick A. Wright, *Agile Auditing: Transforming the Internal Audit Process* (Lake Mary, FL: Internal Audit Foundation, 2019).
10. John R. Graham, et al, "Corporate Culture Evidence from the Field," *Journal of Financial Economics*, Vol 146, Issue 2, November 2022, Elsevier BV
11. Cynthia Cooper, Richard F. Chambers, "Organizational Culture and Ethics Report: Understanding Culture as Culprit, Catalyst, and 21st-Century Differentiator," (Cerritos, CA, AuditBoard, 2023).
12. Jennifer Herrity, "Corporate Culture Examples and Benefits," *Indeed.com*, October 31, 2022.

Chapter 6: Leveraging Enabling Technology

1. John Rodi, Stephen Dabney, "2023 KPMG Audit Committee Insights survey," (KPMG, 2023).
2. "COVID-19: Longer Term Impact on Internal Audit," The Institute of Internal Auditors (2020).
3. "How Audit Departments Deliver Business Value Through Digital Transformation," AuditBoard, 2020.
4. "State of the Internal Audit Profession," PwC, 2019.
5. "What is Agile Auditing? The Benefits of Taking Your Audit Team Agile," AuditBoard, 2020.

6. "State of the Internal Audit Profession," PwC, 2019.
7. Richard F. Chambers, Anand Bhakta, "An AI-Powered Call to Action for Internal Audit," (AuditBoard, 2023).
8. *Gartner Glossary*, Integrated Risk Management (IRM), 2020.

Chapter 7: Agents of Change Aren't Secret Agents

1. "OnRisk 2021: A Guide to Understanding, Aligning, and Optimizing Risk," The Institute of Internal Auditors (2020).
2. Ibid.
3. "PwC's 27th Annual Global CEO Survey: Thriving in an age of continuous reinvention," PwC, 2024.
4. "Seeing through walls to find new horizons, PwC Global Internal Audit Study 2023," PwC, 2023.
5. Ibid.
6. Influence at Work, *Principles of Persuasion*, https://www.influenceatwork.com/ principles-of-persuasion/, Tempe, AZ. Accessed Oct. 9, 2020.
7. TVA Office of Inspector General, Semiannual Report of the Office of Inspector General April 1, 2001 – September 30, 2001, Issued October 31, 2001. Accessed at: https://oig.tva.gov/reports/semi31.pdf
8. Ibid.
9. Nihar Chhaya, "How to Know If Your Humility Has Gone Too Far," *Forbes* (May 7, 2020).
10. Karl Albrecht, PhD, "The Paradoxical Power of Humility: Why humility is underrated and misunderstood," *BrainSnacks*, Jan. 8, 2015.
11. Ibid.
12. Richard F. Chambers, *Trusted Advisors: Key Attributes of Outstanding Internal Auditors* , Internal Audit Foundation (2017).

Chapter 8: Business Acumen

1. Brian Hill, "What Is a Strong General Business Acumen?" Chron. Lynda Moultry Belcher, "Advantages and Disadvantages of Technology Advances," Chron.
2. Dr. Raymond R. Reilly and Dr. Gregory P. Reilly, "Building Business Acumen," *HR West* (December 2009).
3. R. Brodo, "Powerful Business Acumen Skills - 5 Critical Elements," *Advantexe, the power of practice*, https://www.advantexe.com/blog/business-acumen-skills-5- most-important-elements-of-a-learning-journey, Nov. 16, 2015.
4. O. Casselle, "Jobs of the Future Will Require More Technology Acumen," *Digital Adventures*, https:// www.digitaladventures.com/news/2018/2/24/jobs-of-the-future-will-require-more- technology-acumen, 2018.

5. "Workplace Loyalties Change, but the Value of Mentoring Doesn't," *Knowledge at Wharton* podcast, Wharton School of Management, University of Pennsylvania, 2007.
6. Ibid.
7. Lillian T. Eby, Marcus M. Butts, Jaime Durley, and Belle Rose Ragins, "Are bad experiences stronger than good ones in mentoring relationships? Evidence from the protégé and mentor perspective," *Journal of Vocational Behavior* (2010).
8. "The Business Acumen Handbook: Everything You Need to Know to Succeed in the Corporate World," Haines, S., Amazon Digital Services LLC, 2019.
9. Richard F. Chambers, *Trusted Advisors: Key Attributes of Outstanding Internal Auditors*, Internal Audit Foundation (2017).
10. Richard F. Chambers, *The Speed of Risk: Lessons Learned on the Audit Trail*, 2nd Edition, Internal Audit Foundation (2019).

Chapter 9: The Strategic Internal Auditor

1. *Global Internal Audit Standards*, Domain IV: Managing the Internal Audit Function, Principle 9 Plan Strategically, The Institute of Internal Auditors (2024).
2. Accessed at: https://na.theiia.org/translations/PublicDocuments/GPI-Elevating- Internal-Audits-Strategic-Impact-English.pdf
3. Paloma Cantero-Gomez, "The Seven Critical Skills of Successful Strategic Thinkers," *Forbes* (Feb. 5, 2019). Accessed at: https://www.forbes.com/sites/palomacantero- gomez/2019/02/05/the-7-critical-skills-of-successful-strategic- thinkers/?sh=38a455e6656b
4. Ibid.
5. Ibid.
6. Ibid.
7. Ibid.
8. Richard F. Chambers, *Trusted Advisors: Key Attributes of Outstanding Internal Auditors*, Internal Audit Foundation (2017).
9. "The Seven Critical Skills of Successful Strategic Thinkers."
10. Ibid.
11. Ibid.
12. *Trusted Advisors: Key Attributes of Outstanding Internal Auditors.*
13. Brainzooming, "6 Characteristics of Strategic Thinking Skills vs. Tactical Thinking," Apr. 22, 2015. Accessed at: https://brainzooming.com/6-characteristics-of-strategic-thinking-skills/24101/
14. Ibid.

15. "Thinking big with business transformation Six keys to unlocking breakthrough value," Deloitte. Accessed at: https://www2.deloitte.com/content/dam/Deloitte/us/ Documents/process-and-operations/us-sdt-think-big-business-transformation.pdf
16. Ibid.

Chapter 10: On Being Relationship Centric

1. Elaine Houston, "The Importance of Positive Relationships in the Workplace," *PositivePsychology.com* (2020), https://positivepsychology.com/positive-relationships-workplace/
2. Ibid.
3. "Relationship Building Skills: Definitions and Examples," *Indeed.com* (2020), https://www.indeed.com/career-advice/career-development/relationship-building-skills
4. "Emotional Intelligence," *Global Leadership Foundation*, Melbourne, AU, https://globalleadershipfoundation.com/deepening-understanding/emotional-intelligence/
5. Richard F. Chambers, *The Speed of Risk: Lessons Learned on the Audit Trail*, 2nd Edition, Internal Audit Foundation (2019).
6. Richard F. Chambers, Charles B. Eldridge, Paula Park, and Ellen P. Williams, "The relationship advantage: Maximizing chief audit executive success," March 2011, http://www.kornferry.com/ institute/317-the-relationship-advantage-maximizing- chief-auditexecutive-success (accessed November 18, 2016).
7. "How to Know You Are a Change Agent," *NOVARETE*, https://novarete.com/how- to-know-you-are-a-change-agent/#:~:text=A%20Change%20Agent%20is%20 essentially,such%20as%20a%20consultant%20or
8. "Qualities of Effective Change Agents," Michigan State University (2019) https:// www.michiganstateuniversityonline.com/resources/leadership/qualities-of-effective-change-agents/
9. "Seven Essential Traits of a Change Agent," *Enclaria* (2019), https://www.enclaria. com/2019/02/05/seven-essential-traits-of-a-change-agent/
10. "Qualities of Effective Change Agents."
11. Fred C. Lunenberg, "Managing Change: The Role of the Change Agent," *International Journal of Management, Business, and Administration*, Volume 13, Number 1, Sam Houston State University (2010).
12. Chrissy Scivicque, "How to Be Proactive at Work: My 5 Step System," *eatyourcareer. com*, 2010, https://eatyourcareer.com/2010/08/how-be-proactive-at-work-step- system/
13. "Global Internal Audit Standards," Domain II: Ethics and Professionalism, Principle 2 Maintain Objectivity, The Institute of Internal Auditors (2024).

14. "Global Internal Audit Standards," Domain II: Ethics and Professionalism, Principle 2 Maintain Objectivity, Standard 2.1 Individual Objectivity, The Institute of Internal Auditors (2024).
15. "Global Internal Audit Standards," Domain II: Ethics and Professionalism, Principle 2 Maintain Objectivity, Standard 2.2 Safeguarding Objectivity, The Institute of Internal Auditors (2024).
16. "Global Internal Audit Standards," Domain III: Governing the Internal Audit Function, Principle 7 Positioned Independently, The Institute of Internal Auditors (2024).

Chapter 11: The Innovative Mindset

1. Jay Sullivan, "Three Steps To Developing An Innovative Instinct — And The Questions To Ask Yourself To Get There," *Forbes* (2018).
2. Richard F. Chambers, *Trusted Advisors: Key Attributes of Outstanding Internal Auditors*, Internal Audit Foundation (2017).
3. Ibid.
4. Mikael E. Björling, "5 key steps to creating an innovation mindset," *Ericsson Networked Society Lab* (2018), https://www.ericsson.com/en/blog/2018/5/5-key-steps-to-creating-an-innovation-mindset
5. Ibid.
6. Ibid.
7. Daniel Burrus, "Failing is learning: Fail fast to learn faster," *BBN Times*, https://www.bbntimes.com/companies/failing-is-learning-fail-fast-to-learn-faster
8. Ibid.
9. "COVID-19 and the future of business: Executive epiphanies reveal post-pandemic opportunities," *IBM Institute for Business Value*, 2020.
10. Ibid.

Conclusion: Agents of the Future

1. "How to Inspire Change in the Workplace: 10 Ways to Be a Powerful Voice of Change (Even When It Feels Impossible)," *Inspiring Leadership Now* (2020), https:// www.inspiringleadershipnow.com/how-to-inspire-change-workplace/
2. Russell A. Jackson, "Emerging Leaders," *Internal Auditor* (2020).
3. Emily Primeaux, "Emerging Leaders," *Internal Auditor* (2023)